STRATEGIC EXPERIENTIAL FAMILY THERAPY

Dr. Liliana Cabouli

Bloomington, IN  Milton Keynes, UK
authorHOUSE®

AuthorHouse™
1663 Liberty Drive, Suite 200
Bloomington, IN 47403
www.authorhouse.com
Phone: 1-800-839-8640

AuthorHouse™ UK Ltd.
500 Avebury Boulevard
Central Milton Keynes, MK9 2BE
www.authorhouse.co.uk
Phone: 08001974150

© 2007 Dr. Liliana Cabouli. All rights reserved.

No part of this book may be reproduced, stored in a retrieval system, or transmitted by any means without the written permission of the author.

First published by AuthorHouse 2/8/2007

ISBN: 978-1-4259-6350-7 (sc)
ISBN: 978-1-4259-6351-4 (hc)

Printed in the United States of America
Bloomington, Indiana

This book is printed on acid-free paper.

Liliana Cabouli Psy.D;MFT
7968 Arjons drive #D,92126
Tel:(858)610-2080
San Diego, California
92131-1799
http://Seftinstitute.com

Table of Contents

ACKNOWLEDGMENTS	VII
INTRODUCTION	IX
WHEN YOU STOP TALKING THE TALK AND BEGIN WALKING THE WALK	XI
THE GOAL OF THERAPY	1
SYSTEMIC ASSUMPTIONS	15
CHARACTERISTICS, DIFFERENCES, AND SIMILARITIES OF THE INTERGENERATIONAL APPROACH, THE STRUCTURAL APPROACH, AND THE EXPERIENTIAL APPROACH	17
INTEGRATING THE APPROACHES FOR A NEW APPROACH	30
STRATEGIC EXPERIENTIAL FAMILY THERAPY	32
FORMAT OF THE SESSIONS	35
SIX STAGES OF SEFT	37
WORKING WITH COUPLES:	52
ROLE OF THE THERAPIST	53
FUNCTIONAL AND DYSFUNCTIONAL FAMILIES	56
EMOTIONAL EXERCISES	65
EXPERIENTIAL EXERCISES FOR COUPLES.	70
SHOWING VULNERABILITY	73
CREATING INTIMACY BETWEEN FAMILY MEMBERS	78
INDIVIDUAL THERAPY INCORPORATED WITHIN COUPLES WORK	83
CULTURE AND THERAPY	92

SOME RESEARCH	103
MY PHENOMENOLOGICAL RESEARCH STUDY	113
EXAMPLE OF SOME INTERVIEWS	189
TEACHING STRATEGIC EXPERIENTIAL FAMILY THERAPY.	238
REFERENCES CITED	263

Acknowledgments

To all the people I love and connect with throughout my life.

To Timea, who helped me to finish the
book that I was postponing.

To my students, who gave me the support to teach this model.

To my husband and daughter, who are
always there for me and love me.

To my parents, who gave me the gift to work with our
issues to get into a better place in our relationship.

To my father, who taught me that everything is possible.

To my clients: Thank you for letting me into your lives. I
enjoy our encounters, and I learn so much from you.

Thank you for your trust.

Introduction

All through graduate school, I was struggling to identify with one theory model that I would be using in my counseling career. The source of my difficulties is my belief that, if we humans are all so different in our ways, how could one single therapy model help people in a uniform way? How could this uniformity be applied in a culture where so many diverse populations exist? I began searching for a model that encompasses different theories which allows the therapist to be able to mold to each and every client.

When I began to familiarize myself with experiential and strategic therapy, I felt that I had found what I had been searching for. The combination of experiential techniques within the framework of a strategic model allows the therapist to break away from uniformity by allowing the client to experiment on different levels with emotions, gain awareness, and reach a state where the client, in alliance with the therapist, begins the process of change. This model is a powerful force, where constant movement specifically tailored to a particular case is happening within the session and outside of it.

The model is straightforward; it requires commitment and a willingness to change from clients, and it requires commitment and work from the therapist to reach the goals that they set out to attain. There is an enormous power within the exercises which doesn't just teach clients about insight, but also takes them to the next level; awareness. Finally, this is a model that has the capacity to help the client be assertive in getting a good therapist who is comfortable to be out of a comfort zone, who is ready to take risks, who is involved, who can model good communication by being honest in sessions, and who is flexible enough to mold to any situation.

"Dr Liliana Cabouli is the living version of the model. I don't think I have ever met a more insightful, aware, caring, funny, honest, blunt, and vibrant therapist as she is. Besides the major aspects of the model, her personality was another factor that drew me toward the experiential-strategic model. She doesn't just teach the model, but lives by it, which helps one see the effects at hand. Her supervision was beneficial to me on many levels. First, she guided me in experimenting with my own issues, to accept and improve possible transference and countertransference in my future career. Second, she showed me the effects of her exercises on real cases. Third, her feedback helped me to stay on track to make sure that sessions with my clients were heading toward the direction of improvement.

Overall, I greatly enjoy this model and hope to learn more about it, because its effects are astounding. Experiential-strategic therapy works with different populations, different cultures, and a variety of issues."

Timea Tinkei MA.

THIS IS A RESULT-ORIENTED MODEL; BUT TO GET THERE, THERAPISTS NEED TO GO THROUGH MANY STAGES WITH THE CLIENT.

WILL THERAPY BE SUCCESSFUL WHEN YOU ARE WORKING HARDER THAN YOUR CLIENTS?

When I was in school, there was somewhat of a mantra that everyone followed: "Do not work harder than your clients; if they do not care, we should not care." In my experience, clients don't respond to a nonchalant attitude. This is especially true with clients from other cultures; they will feel rejected, and they might perceive the therapist as a cold, indifferent person. It will be very difficult for them to trust someone with that attitude. In the Latino culture, warmth and friendliness is really appreciated. Sometimes, you need to be the one who cares for them and their problems at the beginning stages of therapy; this being a strategy in and of itself. I really recommend showing interest, being genuinely interested, and caring. Do your work with passion and honesty, and you will be a role model to your clients.

I find it important to explain to my clients the process of change in the systemic model, to explain the concept of homeostasis, and to give them hope that they can do it. It is also important for them to be realistic, to know that when change begins it will be uncomfortable and scary, like a medical doctor can be when they explain an illness. They will give a treatment and prognosis. For example, if you have high cholesterol, you need medication, exercise, and diet, "Yes, at the beginning, it is going to be difficult to change those old habits, but in the long run, your health will benefit. If you decide not to follow treatment, I want you to know that you are putting yourself at high risk for a heart attack."

The client is also responsible for their part. A client who is not committed to change will not achieve the goals they want. Therapists are *not* miracle workers. It may be necessary to repeat why they have come and why it is so important that they are present and cooperative. I have no problems with repeating this over and over, and also with reframing their lack of cooperation. If they choose to throw their money away, I will not complain. I may even say things like, "Well, why change? Why bother? If you don't care about your wife cheating on you and you are getting some pleasure out of coming here, I have no problems with that."

Another example might be, "You are saying that your husband treats you badly, but on the other hand, you don't seem to be so concerned about it. It is okay with me if you want to live your life like that, because that is your life, not mine. However, I would like to tell you that the abuse will not stop by itself, and this could get much worse. I am sorry that a smart, beautiful woman like you decided to live the life of a person who settles for less."

"*I am willing to care for you for a while in your struggle, to see if you commit to our work together. I don't like to fail, and without your commitment, I will.*"

In this way, the ego of the client will be challenged, and you will join with him or her in a caring place.

A different way to provoke a client and make them uncomfortable might be to say, "I believe, with all respect, that you are a coward who chooses to be unhappily comfortable, because you are scared to have something and then lose it. You say that you don't have needs, but in reality, you are scared to have what you want, because that would give you responsibilities. This may create anxiety and stress, and to be honest, I am not sure if you can handle that. In the end, it comes down to the old saying: 'No pain, no gain!'"

I do not believe therapy is the process of, "Who works more; the therapist or the client?" or "Who talks more, the therapist or the client?" It is a matter of becoming a team and working toward the goal of family unity, growth, and awareness. This is what I believe in.

TEAM WORK IS THE MAGIC WORD. IT IS A TYPE OF DANCE OF GROWTH AND AWARENESS. Each family plays a different game; that's why each one presents different challenges and a different strategy to help them in the process of change and symptom-relief. Whitaker believes in the battle for structure, as he wants the entire family present in the first session to begin with. I do not agree; all I need is one person to begin with. Little by little, I will work to bring in the rest of the family in order to do a family-of-origin session. I don't care how many people come; sometime I even want them to come alone and work with some issues that can cause resistance to the dynamic and the growth. A non-secrecy policy is the baseline of the treatment. The way I see it is that each person is part of a family system, and that is the way I treat them, and in my experience, they all end up coming. This is a matter of finding the right strategy for each specific couple or family.

Why Clients Understand, But Don't Change

In my model, for change to happen, I create a setting that promotes an orgasmic awareness between the MIND and EMOTIONS. It's an enlightenment that envelops all the senses of your being. It's a sudden, new level of understanding. We all think that, when we have an insight, we understand, or we get "it," but then we go and do the same thing over and over; so the question is, why do we go back and do the same thing if we really understand "it"? It's because we have an emotional system and a mental system, and too often, we emphasize the mental aspect of insight and overlook the importance of emotional understanding. For a client really to grow, we need to create a level of anxiety and intensity. We need to push the client outside their comfort zone. We need to wake up the sleeping emotional system and dismantle the mental guards.

To access the emotional system, a therapist needs to be intense, aware, and have an intense desire to grow. If a therapist doesn't work on their own emotional issues, if a therapist doesn't participate in their own therapy and if a therapist doesn't challenge their own comfort zones and emotional limitations, then they will not be successful in helping the client get out of the "comfort zone." This could cause a therapeutic setback; your clients are not going to get better than you. A lack of desire to see yourself and increase your awareness will affect the level of growth that you can help with or promote to your clients. This model is not for play–it-safe kinds of people, it is for people who have courage and strive for growth.

I recommend that if you are going to work with people from other cultures, you need to have some type of experience of living in another culture, or have traveled outside your own culture to experience being an outsider, and to see what is outside your parameters. When you see outside some given parameters, you will relate to people from other cultures and backgrounds, which will open a new spectrum of experiences.

As I mentioned before, I am from Argentina, and I have traveled extensively to Europe, Asia, South America, Canada, USA, and South Africa. I have lived in Greece, Spain, Miami, and San Diego. In every place, I have had different experiences that have challenged my way of being and my point of view. From each of these, I have grown, suffered, and changed. Every experience became part of who I am, and because of that, I have a real understanding of what it means to be different, to be confused, and to feel that you don't belong. I also experienced how you adapt, embrace and change from the experience of these changes.

I know people have different values, different ideas of what is correct or expected, and different ways of framing life, and I also realize that, besides that, there is a lot in common in human nature, including the need for connection and love, the fear of abandonment and loneliness, the need to be cared for, and the need to be who they are. This is my conclusion, and I understand if people disagree. An idea comes to mind from the Chinese culture, which is based on the notion that, if the pressure for conformity is high, people still want to be themselves and do what they want.

I want to challenge therapists who are scared of not creating a safe environment, or are scared of pushing the client emotionally at the wrong time. I believe that it is important to create a working alliance, not a safe environment. Why? Because it's ridiculous to talk about safety when we know perfectly well that therapy and growth is painful. Who changes during happiness? You grow from pain. You become awake from pain. A good therapist makes the process uncomfortable, but the working alliance remains strong. How do we make a working alliance? How do we convey to our clients that we care about the process enough to be strong, honest, and confrontational?

The answer is in being real as a therapist and having an understanding in your mind that you, as a therapist, will also be growing. Instead of being a codependent, silent ghost, you are going to be part of the system, making selective alliances and taking one side more than another at times; debalancing and pushing. To help the family or the couple tolerate pushing and side-taking, you need a strong, working alliance. This means you will put one hundred percent of yourself into helping them achieve their goals if they work with you and you become in tune with them to understand their needs and the most appropriate way to create movement in each system. We choose a real estate agent to find the best deal and get the most for our money. The client needs to trust that you are interested in finding them the best deal. On the other hand, the therapist believes and transmits this belief that the family has enough resources to change. The therapist needs to be the last to give up for real. It is important to note that this doesn't mean that sometimes, as a strategy, the therapist can say that he or she gave up. In reality, clients need to be the ones who give up first.

Another aspect of this model is that you create a **customized treatment** for each client, depending on their history, their moods, their ways of dealing with conflict, their level of distress, their culture, and their belief systems. As a therapist, you need to be able to finish the first session with a working hypothesis. I challenge therapists who think they need to have twelve sessions with lots of exploring and fishing for useless information for fear of triggering any. The reality of this speaks more about the resistance of the therapist to joining the client than to the client's inability to participate. A client leaving a session prematurely is not a failure of the therapist. It could be that the client wants to hold onto his problems, and they've decided they really want to be like that. It could be a matter of being a coward, or it could be an unconscious choice. A symbol of bad therapy is having a client for months and months, with the client experiencing no change. I would suggest that therapists join the client from day one, so that the client knows that the therapist doesn't buy nonsense.

The bottom line is that the therapist is not going to promote or model indirect communication, or in any way be intimidated by the power of the family or the couple. Why? Because they are going to promote individuation, open communication, and open expression of feelings and ideas from the starting gate.

This model is about facing fears and challenging your own inner limits. It's about confrontation and solutions, NOT going in circles or dancing around loaded issues. This is about real love and connection between people for who they really are, not for who they are pretending to be, for the sake of maintaining a system.

The therapist needs to have power in the system to promote change. If this does not happen, it will not be possible for the system to change, even though the solutions are within the clients. The therapist becomes the light that helps clients and families to see things more clearly and finally make their own choices.

For example, in the case of a family I used to work with, I would suggest that the mother who never followed through on her promises set consequences when the child continues running away and disobeying the rules; and that she should tell the child to continue doing what they're doing, because there was no consequence for what they are doing anyway. The therapist can say, "Why don't we get this clear? Tell the truth: you will not set any consequence for the child's behavior, and that is the truth, so don't threaten if you are not going to follow through. Your kid knows it, so let's get real and be honest, and tell your son that he can do whatever he wants, because there are not going to be consequences."

INDIRECT STRATEGIES.

WHEN UPFRONT IS NOT POSSIBLE AT THE BEGINNING, THEN THE RESOURCE IS TO MANIPULATE THE SYSTEM WITH STRATEGIES

Some people might think that being strategic to get a result is unethical. Sometimes, exaggerating the truth may serve a purpose; such as the disclosure of an exaggerated version of your "rebellious" youth for the purpose of joining with a delinquent teen. The idea is that, if I'm unable to join with the client upfront, I may need to take an indirect approach for the purpose of helping the client open up. It may take longer to be strategic and indirect, but it is more effective. For example, if you are dealing with a person for whom religion is more of a crutch because of past trauma, you may consider being more subtle and understanding before challenging some of this person's distorted beliefs. Let it be noted that in no way am I condemning religion, or saying that religion is a crutch for anyone who "believes." For example, let's say a religious mother uses her religion to reject her gay son, and so therefore, every conversation ends up with the mother using the Bible or God to justify her rejection and conditional love, despite causing her son severe emotional pain. In this situation, the therapist would need to be careful and strategic in order to achieve the goal of creating a connection between the son and mother. For example, the therapist might look for a biblical "escape clause" that relieves the mother of the burden of feeling caught in the middle of making a choice between disavowing her faith and accepting her son. This mother may feel that she is in a dilemma, and she may fear the responsibility of choosing between God and her son. One such mother I encountered was able to accept her son on the basis of a biblical clause that allowed for this mother to accept non-believers. As long as the son was willing to claim non-believer status, the mother felt that she could accept him, because this clause did not create any conflict with her beliefs, and was in accordance with her faith.

If a client wants to change, but the message is, "I want to change, but I don't want to change" (in other words "I don't want to pay the price to change"), what can a therapist do with this double bind? For example, a client might say, "I want to lose weight, but I don't want to stop eating," or "I want to have muscles, but I don't want to work out." With this double-bind a therapist has the option of being honest and confronting the client about their unrealistic and irrational expectations, but most likely, this will not effectively help this client achieve their goal of "losing weight" or "gaining muscles." **Behind the statement, "I want to change, but I don't want to change," could be fear of failure, fear of what it could came could be worst that today's problems or fear of sacrifice and being out of their comfort zone.**

A more strategic approach might be to be indirect and compare the client to others like saying you understand how painful it is and how you used to have clients with the same problem that chose to lose weight and are so happy right now.

This manipulation of the system could be done in different ways that would be specifically designed for each case. This is why, when working with this integrative, strategic approach, it is important to have group peer supervision or a supervisor trained in this approach, until the repertoire of the therapist is big enough to handle different types of clients and problems.

MY IDEA IS, WHATEVER IT TAKES TO ACHIEVE THE GOAL, I WILL DO IT, WITH MY ETHICAL STANDARDS IN MIND, BECAUSE THE WELFARE OF MY CLIENTS COMES FIRST.

ADVICE GIVING

How do you give advice without giving advice? And, by the way, what is the problem with the therapist giving advice?

Restate the client's problem by using a sarcastic metaphor for what they are actually doing. Suggest that they continue this activity, which, in reality, makes no sense.

Suggesting that the mother continue her nonsensical behavior by restating the observation of what she is doing is a strategic way of increasing awareness with humor and emphasis.

Advice-giving is always an option for a therapist; however, it is never the only way to go. In a case of abuse, the therapist can have a standpoint that is more definite. On the other hand, my stand regarding advice is that it would not hurt when someone is completely lost, or if someone had no parents to guide them when growing up, or for people who are not educated. It is highly recommended in cases where you are working with minority clients (Hispanic and Asian). They expect that from you. In Spanish, "counseling" means "advice-giving."

I am not scared to give advice regarding parenting skills, or relationships where a severe power imbalance is occurring, such as cases of very unhealthy relationships, domestic violence; people who are struggling to find a committed relationship, and as a strategy to imbalance the system.

"I AM A NEW THERAPIST. HELP!"

What a problem: "I am a new therapist, and I don't know what to do, and I feel helpless, because I am lost and don't know what I am doing, and I am scared, and I am probably not doing my job, because people don't change." This is the phrase I hear over and over from students and new professionals. They want a little guidance. And what is wrong with that?

When I finished my career in Argentina, I had my supervisor for three years who guided me and taught me how to let myself be creative. I am so thankful to her, because instead of sending me contradictory messages, she gave me the hope of trusting the process, being real as a therapist, and creating, step by step, new ways to get closer to the goal of changing dysfunctional systems. She encouraged my creativity, improved my thinking process, and was very honest with me. I knew she cared about my clients and cared about me becoming the best therapist that I could be.

I would like to give all of you some inspiration in regards to *your* becoming the best therapist that you can be. Risk is part of it, as is having your mind thinking fast enough and your observation skills develop until a point where it is natural for you to observe and create hypotheses very fast. The most important thing is THAT YOU MAKE YOUR MOVEMENTS WISELY ENOUGH TO PLAY THE GAME OF EACH FAMILY, COUPLE, OR INDIVIDUAL. ALSO, THAT YOU BEGIN TO CHANGE THE RULES IF THEY'RE NOT WORKING. ALL OF YOUR MOVEMENTS HAVE A PURPOSE TOWARD YOUR GOAL.

In order to achieve this, you need training, you need experience with stop-feedback analysis, you need to have a capacity to take feedback, and most importantly, you need the drive for self-growth and awareness.

If you agree, this book and this model are for you.

Let's get real: every therapist calls the same things different names. They fight from safe environments for self-differentiation, as if someone has the real truth. In my experience, this is a matter of semantics, and human nature is more than that. I want to be concrete and get to the point; I want less philosophy, and more results.

A LITTLE BACKGROUND OF OTHER MODELS

This review of literature begins with a discussion of the basic assumptions of systemic approaches, followed by descriptions of the models and a contrast of the similarities and differences of the three models that are part of the integrative SEFT. Finally, the integrative approach is presented and described.

SYSTEMIC ASSUMPTIONS

Systemic theories are influenced by cybernetics. A number of points arise that are pertinent to systemic work with families. They are classified as systems with a focus on family members interacting, relating, transacting, and organizing around one another. Bertalanffy (1968), a biologist, proposed a general systems theory in which he conceptualized that changes occur as a result of the interactions of the components of an organism. Growth and change occur as a result of systems interacting with other systems. Waxlike, Bovine, and Jackson (1967) defined systems as combinations of interacting components with identifiable boundaries that compose wholes. Another property of systems is that, when one component of a system changes, change occurs in the symptoms.

Systems have a number of important properties. First, systems are nonsummative, which means that the whole is more than the sum of the parts. Second, no matter where one enters the system, the same process will result. This property, termed equifinality, suggests that a focus on behavioral patterns is considered more important than a focus on individual topics. Third, circular causality refers to the idea that any behavior or event in a system is both the cause and the effect, and is reciprocally related. The idea of circular causality contradicts the linear cause-and-effect idea found in traditional psychotherapy. A fourth property of systems is that they continually receive information from their environment. A fifth concept of systems theory is homeostasis (Waxlike et al. 1967). Homeostasis refers to maintenance of the status quo. Family members tend to behave in ways that protect the steady state. Homeostasis is generally maintained through the process of negative feedback. A negative consequence of this process may occur when a family member improves, and the disturbance reappears elsewhere in the family. On the other hand, when families maintain equilibrium between change and stability, both the families and their individual members function adaptively throughout the life cycle. Patients are the "symptom bearers," and their symptoms maintain homeostasis in families. Symptoms can therefore be viewed as part of the clients' system and are considered interpersonal. In traditional psychotherapy, symptoms are believed to reside within the clients. In other words, the symptoms and concomitant problems are intrapsychological (Auerswald 1969).

Characteristics, Differences, and Similarities of the Intergenerational Approach, the Structural Approach, and the Experiential Approach

Characteristics, differences, and similarities of intergenerational, structural, and experiential approaches are discussed, followed by a review of some of the most important concepts and techniques of these approaches to family therapy. The section concludes with a description and explanation of SEFT. The basic family systems assumption is that the family is an important emotional system; it shapes and continues to determine the course and outcome of our lives. Because the family is our greatest resource, it is also our greatest potential source of stress. The system interaction is circular. If a person changes his or her predictable emotional input and reaction, the system puts pressure on the person to return to previous or more "normative" patterns of interaction. For example, the more distance between spouses, the closer one spouse is going to be to the third point of the triangle. This is another important concept. When emotional intensity is too strong and the pull toward fusion is high, family members cut themselves off from the relationship. However, cutting oneself off physically or emotionally does not end the emotional process. Differentiation, the main concept of the Bowen theory, describes a state of self-definition that does not rely on the need for acceptance by others for one's own beliefs. Bowen's family systems therapy is not defined by or restricted to the number of family members who attend therapy sessions (Bowen 1974). Bowen's intergenerational approach is based on the notion that, if one person changes, all others in emotional contact with that person would make compensatory changes. The main point of this approach is that individual symptoms and problems are placed in systemic context and explored in terms of relationships. Discussion focuses on overall patterns in the network. Individuals get close to another person and then go back to their own goals and life. Even though different cultures have different ways of expressing emotional maturity, they find culturally acceptable and respectful ways to be themselves.

Detriangling is another important aspect of this approach. Triangles are dysfunctional, in that they offer stabilization through diversion, rather than through resolution of the problem between the twosome. In healthy triads, each relationship is independent of the other two. The therapist is a coach or mentor who guides the client to differentiation.

Emotional anxiety tends to lead to fusion, and may lead an individual to attempt to control or dominate others. Autonomy may be abandoned, due to fear of losing the love of family members. Indeed, women in our society have, for a long time, been cut off from their needs in order to be emotionally connected with others. Emotional maturity is observed when people can think, plan and follow their own values while being emotionally present with others. They do not live reactively by the cues of those close to them, and are not focused on winning approval, attacking others, intellectualizing, being emotionally defensive, or manipulating relationships to achieve control. Taking an "I" position is important to a differentiated person. This means making a statement without being offensive or defensive of one's thoughts or feelings regarding a certain subject (Bowen 1978). On the other hand, Framo's intergenerational approach (1991) bases his approach on Bowen's concept and further elaborates on other ideas. He believes that culture is a factor to consider, and his theory is based on attachment theory, which is different than Bowen's natural science and biology paradigm. Both Framo and Bowen are interest in concept of self-differentiation.

There are differences between structural, strategic, and the Bowen and Framo family therapy approaches. Bowen views symptoms as unresolved family problems passed down through generations. Problems are inherent to the system, rather than to the person. Change is sought through changing relationships with others, achieving a higher level of differentiation, and adjusting the most important triangle—including the couple. Maladaptive behavior is the result of a multigenerational transition process, in which progressively lower levels of differentiation are transmitted from one generation to the next (Bowen 1978). Framo (1981) believes that symptoms are generated in a pathological family and are frequently the outcome of irrational role assignments, the blurring of generational boundaries, family trauma, the maintenance of symptoms for system purposes and the emotional overburdening of the child,(Framo 140)

In structural theory, the symptom, or the maladaptive behavior, is the result of an inflexible family structure that prohibits the family from adapting to maturational and situational stressors in a healthy way (Minuchin, Lee, and Simon 1996). For example, a symptom exhibited by a child can serve to diffuse stress when there is conflict between parents. The role of communication in maladaptive behavior is emphasized with a particular focus on how communication is used to increase control in a relationship. The symptom is interpersonal rather than intrapsychic, and is defined as a strategy used to control relationships only if other strategies have failed. Struggles of control become pathological when one or both parties deny the intention of controlling the other person (Haley 1985).

The role of the therapist in Bowen's model is that of an emotionally detached coach, a supervisor, and a teacher (Liddle, Breunlin, and Schwartz 1988). Bowen believes that education must precede change, and that the client becomes a systems expert. Framo (1981) proposes that the therapist needs to have some control over the sessions. He states that in the diagnostic sessions, he abstains from making interventions and has a conversational style that consists of questioning, empathizing, challenging, stage directing, confronting, balancing, supporting, reflecting and sharing some of his own experiences. Framo tends to work in co-therapy. In contrast with Bowen's concept of a therapist, and more similar to Framo's concept, a structural therapist is an active, directive, challenging therapist in an expert position (Minuchin, Lee, and Simon 1996).

The first goal of Bowen's therapy is to reduce the level of anxiety and alleviate symptoms (Bowen 1978). Anxiety is part of every system, and may turn to dysfunction in the family. Processes, such as projection and triangulation, are means of diffusing anxiety. If therapists coach clients on how to avoid fusion, the theory assumes symptoms will be alleviated. Framo's goal is the family-of-origin encounter that produces change in the individual, the marital and parental subsystem, and the family-of-origin system, because clients relate better with parents and siblings, and they are more able to relate with spouses and children (Framo1981).

Another difference between systems and traditional therapies is how symptoms are conceptualized. In systems theory, identified patients are the "symptom bearers," and their symptoms maintain homeostasis in families. Symptoms are in the clients' system and are considered interpersonal. In traditional psychotherapies, symptoms are believed to reside within the clients. In other words, the symptoms and concomitant problems are intrapsychological. In structural therapy, the goal is to restructure the family (Minuchin and Fishman 1981). This involves restructuring the family's system of transactional rules, breaking up triangles and coalitions, shifting power, and establishing boundaries. The last may be accomplished by strengthening the parental executive subsystem. It is also important to create an effective hierarchical structure. Therapy may address short-term goals—for example, targeting presented problems by using techniques from other theories, such as cognitive-behavioral therapy.

Bowen (1978) stated that, in order to promote change, the client must learn to distinguish between thinking and feeling. Through this process, clients can resolve relationship problems by lowering anxiety and increasing self-focus. The main mechanism of change in this model is awareness of and ability to regulate one's role in interpersonal processes. Part of this process involves developing a personal relationship with everyone in the extended family in order to dissolve the emotional energy. Change in a triangle, for example, causes change in the entire family system. Family therapy with individuals is based on the premise that, if one person in the family achieves a higher level of differentiation of self, other members of the family will do the same. Therapy is not necessary with the whole family in the room, and it is not sufficient to see only the nuclear family; the awareness of the entire family is necessary (Bowen 1974).

In the structural approach, behaviors are changed by opening alternative patterns of family interaction that can modify the family system (Minuchin et al 1996). This involves activating dormant patterns. When functional transactions are activated, they will be reinforced. Therapists join and accommodate to the style of the family, and they look for areas of flexibility. Through the joining process, families come to trust their therapists, and they come to respond to interventions that promote change. Increased stress unbalances the homeostatic balance. This creates a structural transformation and misunderstanding of the power hierarchy of the family. In this sense, Haley shares the ideas of Minuchin et al.

The perspective of Minuchin et al (1996) includes clear boundaries, hierarchies where the parental subsystems work, and clear boundaries within the sibling subsystem. There are no rigid triangles, alliances, or cross-generational alliances when the power is in the parental subsystem, communication is open, and there is flexibility in the family to adjust to different developmental stages. Healthy families struggle. It is not the absence of problems that makes them normal; it is the functional family structure.

Bowen therapy is long-term (Bowen 1978). First, therapists reduce anxiety in the system, detriangle the clients' family of origin, and help to develop differentiated selves. Sessions are educative, cognitive, and controlled. Interpretations, self-disclosure by therapists, and transference are avoided. Clients are encouraged to talk to the therapist in a calm, factual manner. Therapists encourage clients to detriangle by developing a meaningful and well-differentiated relationship with the therapist in the presence of other family members. Clients are taught about family systems and their dynamics, and they explore current problems in the context of the family multi-generational transmission process. Thus, clients can better understand and change their systems. Therapists use the genogram and the family of origin as tools during the middle stage of therapy. With awareness gained from the genogram, clients can begin to understand how to change their dysfunctional behavior. At this point, they are asked to contact family members through telephone calls, letters, or photo-album reviews. Staying in contact with families while remaining emotionally detached or neutral increases a client's level of self-differentiation. Framo's (1982) intent is to create the family of origin conference. Those meetings create an opportunity for corrective experience, in which discoveries are made in regard to information about the family, which helps to integrate splits and decrease projection. Framo and Bowen differ in the fact that Framo brings the family to the office while Bowen sends the client to their homes.

Structural therapists go through three overlapping steps during the therapy process (Minuchin and Fishman 1981). First, therapists develop therapeutic systems by joining the family in a position of leadership. They blend with families by tracking and mimesis (the goal is to ensure that the family understands that the therapist is working with them). Next, therapists evaluate the structure, transactional patterns, power hierarchies, alignments, and boundaries within the family. With this information, therapists create maps with which they can identify diagnoses and set goals. The final step is to restructure the family using different interventions, including unbalancing, boundary making, restructuring techniques, facilitating enactments, and reframing. Structural therapists view a symptom as the result of a structure that cannot meet the developmental needs of the members. The role of the therapist in structural therapy is basically to take charge, show expertise, and be directive, active, and rarely neutral. Bowenian therapists are also directive, but must remain totally neutral and function as a coach or a teacher. Minuchin therapists also act as educators. Change occurs in structural therapy by altering the system (Minuchin et al. 1996). In Bowenian therapy, change occurs by obtaining an understanding of intergenerational patterns, detriangulating family members, achieving self-differentiation, and avoiding cutoffs between the members of the family of origin. Therefore, in Bowenian therapy, goals are achieved through insight.

Framo's thepary is about a new corrective experience with family of origin that helps clients relate to their own spouse's in a more realistic way (Framo 1970).

Experiential theory is described by Whitaker (1976) as the chilling effect of theory on intuition and creativity; therefore, he recommended giving up theory as soon as possible. It is not emphasis on theory; the therapist should be spontaneous, real, and involved. Vitality in a therapist is one of the most important characteristics. Whitaker believed that people are capable of discovering their own directions in life. These ideas contrast Bowen's idea of a therapist coach and detached calm presence, and they are closer to the structural therapist concept as an active directive professional. The belief is that the therapist can be a real person. The therapist can teach the family to be the same; in a way, the therapist is a role model. Experiential therapists are people who believe in themselves (Whitaker 1975). "By being, as nearly as possible, a total person, rather than playing the role of the therapist, the atmosphere encourages all members to participate as total personalities" (Kempler 1965,58). Satir (1972) expressed that the goal of family therapy is to communicate clearly between family members what they feel and think about themselves and others. Whitaker believed that personal growth is related to family unit and vice versa. The sense of belongingness and freedom are both important. This belief is important in the structural approach and in intergenerational approach. Experiential and intergenerational approaches are both concerned with differentiation, and they believe that if one can be close to the family, one cannot individualize; meaning close as different or fused or cut off. Experiential clinicians think that effective family therapy requires powerful interventions and that it is promoting an emotional experience in the treatment between family members. In contrast to structural therapy, experiential therapy is more concerned with the welfare of the individual than that of the family, but is also concerned with the concepts of boundaries and hierarchies. Experiential therapy wants the parents to be in their role as parents. Satir also talked about the importance of joining and understanding, that caring and acceptance were the keys to help people to overcome the fear of change that means going into the unfamiliar. Experiential family therapy is designed to change families by changing family members' concepts that share with Bowen's intergenerational therapy. On the other hand, structural therapy changes the family members by changing the family system. Experiential therapy comes from the phenomenological approach that proposes the idea that self-expression and individual freedom can undo the debilitating effects of culture and advocate craziness and an irrational experience as the goal of therapy (Whitaker 1975).

Experiential therapy shares in common some concepts with Framo's intergenerational therapy; the role of the therapist is not so far apart, and the importance of having new emotional experience is in both theories important as a paradigm for change.

CONCEPTS AND TECHNIQUES OF THE STRUCTURAL-STRATEGIC APPROACH

Structural therapy relies on some important concepts that are defined and explained in this section. The process of *joining* allows the therapist to enter and blend with the family system. Through this way, the members of the family begin to trust the therapist before he or she attempts to change the system (Minuchin 1981). *Reframing the problem* is a technique that helps a family perceive its problem in an alternate way, giving the symptoms another meaning, and thereby enabling the family to respond to their difficulties in different ways. The main goal is to detriangle the IP by first unbalancing the system and then restructuring it (Minuchin 1981). *Enactment* is a technique in which the therapist directs family members to interact with one another in the session in order to encourage risk-taking regarding new forms of interacting (Minuchin and Fishman 1981). Some types of enactments include changes in hierarchies, paradoxical interventions, and homework assignments. *Boundary-making* (Minuchin and Fishman) is a technique that is used to challenge the dysfunctional structure of the family. Three interrelated features define the dysfunctional family structure: (a) either weak or rigid boundaries (enmeshment or disengagement, respectively); (b) an inverted hierarchy, in which the child controls his or her parents, rather than the other way around; and (c) transactions involving triangulation, detouring, and cross-generational coalitions.

Questioning family assumptions is a technique used to challenge the family's perception of reality. The task of the therapist is to offer the family alternative views of reality. *Paradoxical communication* is any manner of communicating that is contradictory, similar to a double-bind. The main idea is to use a client's resistance in a positive way (for example, a couple that fights often might be instructed to argue at least two times every evening; Haley 1985). *Ordeals that are unpleasant* include tasks that the client must perform when a symptom occurs. For example, a man who dislikes his mother-in-law might be instructed to buy an expensive present for her when they have a fight (Haley). *Restraining strategies* include warning the family not to change (Haley). *Positioning strategies* consist of exaggerating the family's negative interpretation of the situation (Haley).

INTERGENERATIONAL WORK PROCESS OF COACHING

Intergenerational work does not rely on techniques; rather, it is a process of teaching family systems to the clients and sending them home to learn how to deal with their own family in a more differentiated way. The process of coaching has been described by Bowen (1978) as a process that involves three stages:

1. *Engagement and systemic mapping—helping clients to see their problems in a systemic way, that is, to shift focus from the self or others to a view of self-with-others;*

2. *Learning about the system and one's role in it—the stage of planning that happens when a client's anxiety is low enough to discuss how personal thoughts and feelings fit into family patterns and give some consideration to possible changes and effects. Gathering information for the genogram changes the focus of guilt and blame to a more objective researcher position. As the coachee begins to observe and listen at a family gathering instead of participating in his or her usual role, he or she can experience shifts in his position.*

3. *The main work—once the clients begin to think about themselves and their families and make initial changes in position, they need to begin putting in more effort. At this moment, the coach should pay attention to the relationship interactions to have a grasp of cultural norms of the family, race, economic status, religion, and education in order to be aware of the principle triangles.*

The main goals of this treatment are to lower the reactivity, create a genogram, increase insight of the multigenerational transmission process, detriangle the family, open a closed system, increase self-differentiation, and take an "I" position (Bowen 1978).

Framo's (1970) intergenerational approach is concerned with bringing the family to the office. He works with couples for a few sessions, then he sends them to groups of couples and prepares them for the meeting with their family of origin. This occurs at the end of the treatment, with the idea of helping client's deal with issues involving their parents and siblings.

Framo (1970) stated that his technique with a couple depends on the problem that is presented, but he focuses on changing the rules of the relationship. he teaches them how to fight, he uses interpretations; challenging and eliciting of effects. He also uses paradoxical interventions and homework assignments.

THE EXPERIENTIAL APPROACH: CONCEPTS AND STRATEGIES

Certain concepts and techniques are useful to understand the experiential approach. These are augmenting the family's despair, using drama, and using metaphors:

> 1. *Augment the despair of the family (Whitaker 1975). This is useful when utilized with the person who is in the scapegoat position. For example: "Do you think that if you continue being depressed and not doing schoolwork, you will improve your parents' relationship?" The therapist treats children as children and not as peers. The therapist is supportive, but sets strong limits. The therapist connects people to their own emotions, helps family members to express how much they like and love each other, instead of how much they struggle with each other, and increases understanding and direct communication.*

2. *Use drama. The therapist directs the family to act out scenes or role-play what might otherwise be repressed or difficult to get in touch with (Whitaker 1975).*

3. *Use metaphors. The therapist uses symbols, stories, or images to indirectly input information or suggestions into the family system (Whitaker 1975).*

According to experiential therapists, family problems arise from the smothering of emotions and impulses. The goal of therapy is to liberate these impulses. For Whitaker (1975), the initial phases of therapy are crucial. The first phase is referred to as the battle for structure, and during this phase, the therapist is in charge. Using humor, teasing, and his personality to accentuate irrational thoughts and behaviors to the point of absurdity, Whitaker increases stress and anxiety in order to precipitate change. In these ways, the therapist "functions as a stress activator, a growth expander, and a creativity stimulator" (Whitaker and Keith 1981, 208).

Both provocative and evocative, experiential family therapy is designed to unfreeze family interactions. Its focus is the immediacy of relating that is fostered among family members. The role of the therapist is like that of a coach, a grandfather, or grandmother (Withaker 1976, Withaker 1975); a very active role that is more similar to the structural role of therapy (Minuchin, and Fishman 1981) and to the intergenerational Bowenian concept of a therapist—but not neutral, more involved. The concept of maturation is similar to the Bowenian concept of self-differentiation in the sense that there is development of separateness and identity, although it is achieved in a different way. Development is viewed as a result of being in touch with one's feelings and values to the point that thoughts and feelings can be communicated effectively.

INTEGRATING THE APPROACHES FOR A NEW APPROACH

Although these three models of therapy share the common denominator of producing change, they achieve change through different paths. In this integrative model, structural, intergenerational, strategic, and experiential work together and use their differences as complementary pieces at various points in the therapy. The main theory is experiential, because the relationship between clients and therapist is very important. The experience the therapist has with the clients is used to promote new experience and increase self-esteem; growth and congruence are one of the ultimate goals. For this study, five stages of the therapy will be described; in each stage, the therapist has different roles and goals. In other words, the therapist begins as a structural therapist (Minuchin and Fishman 1981), working with the entire family, and continues as a facilitator who helps clients to express emotions and communicate clearly (Whitaker 1975, 1976). The therapist ends as a neutral coach (Bowen 1974, 1978), working with both parents, or the most motivated parent, to help clients to gain insight into intergenerational patterns. The differences between the approaches become individual parts of the new approach, each one influencing and helping to achieve the second-order changes, which is the goal of systemic therapy (i.e., helping to promote growth and individuation in members of the system). These two goals are interconnected and create a circle where individuation and growth produce change in the family structure; the change in the family structure will create growth and individuation in members.

Strategic Experiential Family Therapy

The most important point in this systemic integrational approach is that the client is the family, even if working with one client, and the role of the therapist changes in different stages of the process from more active and involved to more calm and outside the emotional system. The paths used to promote change in the family are as follows:

1. A new emotional experience between family members, which promotes self-growth, congruence, open communication, intimacy, and increased self-esteem. If parents are not alive, role-playing, letters, and imaginary guidance can still be used. It will be used to promote a new sense of awareness that will increase self-esteem and create a new relationship with themselves that will enhance their relationships with others.

2. The understanding of family patterns that are impacting effective parenting. Grandparents are brought to the session, if they are available, to experience them differently and finish unresolved business. They become aware, themselves, of the multigenerational transmission process. They open up to their adult children and increase intimacy and trust with them.

> *SEFT has a protocol to follow but it is also customized to the level of acceptance and flexibility of the parents.*
>
> *Framo (1981) stated that the parents in the sessions are not the same; the client interjects, and the dissonance produces the opportunity for change. An important factor would be the role of apology; for example, a parent's apology for maltreatment can lead to an improvement in the client's self-esteem (Framo 1981).*
>
> 3. *The parents learn to set boundaries and accept that they have authority (Minuchin and Fishman 1981). If they have difficulties assuming the leadership position, they learn it through the therapist teaching parenting skills and modeling. One can say that the therapist, in a way, persuades the parents to buy into the leadership/authority role.*

Generally speaking, families might be described as stuck, and may become symptomatic because they have difficulty appreciating their strengths. Instead, they focus on what is lacking. In other words, change is achieved through breaking the negative, nonproductive cycle which emphasizes a new way of interacting and communicating; more freely and open. The family begins to experience the relationships between its members in a new way. Blame and scapegoating are not needed any more. Change is achieved through a modification of the family system, through which individuation and self-esteem is built. On the other hand, when individuals change for the better, the family system is also helped. Change happens inside and outside the therapy setting, and is a circular process with ups and downs; the trend is what matters. Chaos and instability are part of the process, and the therapist needs to tolerate these, in addition to trusting the process. Therefore the therapist needs to be honest with his or her feelings and tolerate confrontation. This therapy is not pity-based, and is about believing in the resourcefulness of people and families. It is a therapy of connecting people in a way they haven't experienced connection before; achieving this by helping people become who they really are. With knowing who they really are comes the ability to have true intimacy and connection. For that reason, it is required that therapists have had experiential therapy themselves and have learned how to be comfortable with their emotions, as well as emotions of others. Therapists should be able to handle and be comfortable with direct communication and be willing to take risks: de-balancing, provoking, eliciting, pushing, and tolerating intense anxiety. When we begin to dance with our clients to their music, we may see that the dance changes along with the music.

Let me explain to you this with an example:

Client: You are boring me. I wouldn't be here if it weren't for the system making me come, and I'm tired of everybody telling me what to do, and it's you white people who are the reason for the situation we're in.

Therapist: Well, you're boring me, too, and since when did the color of your skin become an excuse for why you're not doing what you should be doing? You should be proud of your color, not ashamed of it or using it as an excuse to hide behind, like a coward. You know, what I really think is that you need to be bored with yourself and get tired of yourself and all of your excuses for not doing what you really want to do.

Client: You know what? Fuck you and everybody who wants to tell me what to do, because I don't need anybody, and if everybody just left me and my baby alone and stopped telling me what to do, we would be just fine.

Therapist: Anybody can say what you are saying. Those words are so easy and convenient and sound so powerful, but in reality, you are hiding behind those words, because it's easier for you to get all these people around you to do things for you than for you to take a chance and do it for yourself. You are terrified, and you know that if you try to do something by yourself, you might fail, and you don't know if you could handle that.

Client: Now I'm really mad, and I don't care what you say.

Therapist: That's good. Because it's better to be mad than depressed and bored. Let your anger drive you to do what you need to do for yourself.

Client: Can I go now?

Therapist: Don't you see that I'm standing here by the door waiting for you to leave?

Client: Well, I can't make it next week—I mean the following week, because it's Thanksgiving.

Therapist: Okay, so next week, same time?

Client: Okay.

Format of the Sessions

The sessions are open to every person in the family who is willing to participate in the process, when both therapist and client have decided that the time is right. Extended family members are invited to some of the sessions. For example if the couple is stuck, and the therapist understands that the problem is related to issues with parents or sibling(s) from the family of origin, then extended family members are invited. The first goal for these intergenerational sessions is to confront unresolved issues and have an open, congruent, honest, non-reactive communication, verbally and emotionally, and create a new, corrective emotional experience. If clients do become reactive, the therapist will let it happen, by which he or she will promote resolution. I encourage all therapists not to fear such reactivity, but to guide to it confidently. The second goal is related to setting boundaries between the nuclear family and the extended family. It is important to explain to families that the loyalty they built is more important in the close family than in the extended one.

Parents of adult children are very important to this model. If I can work with two adult generations, I will do it.

A lot of parents have the same issues as their kids. If I could impact the system from these two generations to change multigenerational transmission processes, I would. Some parents come once a month (two hours session) for a period of time to work with my clients (their adult kids) on their issues. This type of work accelerates the process of change incredibly. I have a lot of parents coming from out of state . When they are out of the country, I set up a one to-three-week schedule, like two hours, three times a week. This work requires a minimum eight hours.

I don't care if both parents don't come; if I have one, I do my job because I assume that this is going to impact their immediate system.

If parents are unavailable or deceased, the work would involve the use of the empty chair technique, imaginary guidance, and letters to the parents (refer to the technique section).

The sessions are divided in two. In the first part, all family members are present; in the second part, the adult parents are present without the children. The goal here is to set boundaries between adults and children and to work on dysfunctions in the marital or parental subsystem. In the case of a single-parent home, the same rule would be applied. When working with couples, this model sets up sessions where either the individual, family of origin, or both partners are present. First the therapist works with the couple until things get better, or if things get stuck. Then therapy can move onto the next level, where they do family-of-origin work, through which they can work unresolved issues.

It is advised to be very careful to make the parents understand that they need a change in the system in order to improve the family function, and the symptoms of one or more children are the result of a family that is not functionally structured; therefore, we don't change kids, we change families.

In the case where we have a couple coming to therapy, it would be important to have some family sessions to see the dynamics of the system and how children are involved or triangled in the marriage to set boundaries.

SIX STAGES OF SEFT

There are six stages in SEFT: (a) blending with the family, or the motivational stage; (b) reframing the problem as a family problem, or the shared-responsibility stage; (c) rebalancing and setting boundaries, which is the beginning of the change; (d) the power-struggle stage; (e) the emotional stage of intergenerational connection and (f) the insight-oriented stage. Each is described below.

Stage 1: Motivation. The first stage of SEFT is joining and blending with the family, the motivational stage. Joining and blending are important steps toward making the family feel uncomfortably motivated to change. In this stage, the therapist searches for information and asks questions about the symptoms and period of time when symptoms began. It is important to respect the family, to help them to trust the resources they have, to learn about the culture of the family, and to observe dynamics, processes, hierarchies, and closeness or distance between family members. The therapist assumes the role of the expert (a role very important for minority populations); yet nice, loving, and warm, otherwise known in Latino culture as "personalismo" (McGoldrick, Giordano, and Pearce 1996). The therapist shows caring and genuine interest in a relaxed manner. For example, with respect to working with Latino cultures, these individuals highly value emotions and honesty. A very cold, impersonal, mind-oriented structure type of therapy could be seen as non-empathetic, and the connection could fail. Latino clients expect therapists to give advice and to teach them concepts that would be useful and important to them. Failing to do so could be interpreted as unhelpful counseling.

This stage begins on the phone, when the client calls you to set an appointment. Let me give you an example of what I do:

Client: Hello, can I talk to Dr. Cabouli

Dr. C: This is she, how can I help you?

Client: Well, I was looking to set an appointment with you; my son is misbehaving.

Dr. C: Okay, Let me tell you the way I work, to see if I am a good fit for your family.

Client: Okay.

Dr. C: Well, first I want you to know that I am from Argentina. How do you feel working with someone from another culture?

Client: That is perfect for me.

Dr. C: Okay. Second, I only work with very motivated clients; people who are willing to put in one hundred percent in therapy to achieve their goals. By the way, I put one hundred percent into my part. Third, I am a straightforward person, so I don't go around and around, because it would cost you a lot of money to afford me if I did that. I do not spend a lot of time joining with you and your family. And fourth, I don't believe in individual problems, I believe in system problems. If your son is struggling, I need to see the whole family to assess what the system is that needs to change to stop needing that problem. So you are involved?

Client: I would love that. I am tired of those therapists who say nothing and write on paper.

Dr. C: Well, good, we are on the same page.

Ninety percent of the time, people are happy and enthusiastic with my offer, and they are looking forward to meeting with me.

Minuchin (1972) explained that "joining" means becoming part of the family, or one might say becoming part of the family for a period of time until the family can resolve their problems on their own. They would be very open to the therapist regarding improvement, and they would tell the therapist when therapy is no longer needed. For the sake of the family, it is important to show genuine interest and become a team player. Normalizing them would be appropriate. The whole idea can be condensed in this phrase:

"I'm here with this family to help them in every way I can; to guide them and let them guide me, seeking their best interest; to help them in the process of change, so the family can be happier. I know they can, because they are a great, resourceful family; let us work together."

The following are examples of interventions in this period:

> Therapist: I will do my best, and I ask you to do the same, so we can resolve your problems. I know we will find a way. I have had cases in the past very similar to yours, and things were resolved very well. Don't worry, this is not terrible. All families have issues, and I can see a lot of strengths in yours. I think you are very brave to come and ask for help. This is very healthy.

It is very important to build cultural sensitivity, meaning to embrace the culture of your clients and become a part of it. It is also important to be casual and outgoing and to make jokes. The whole idea is to make them feel welcome, accepted, and safe. When working with Latino clients, *simpatia* (McGoldrick et al. 1996) in the therapist is an important quality to build. *Simpatia,* (Szapocznik et al. 1989) means being casual, non-threatening, open, relaxed, honest, humorous, trustworthy, and comfortable with oneself. In the Latino culture, too much formalism can be seen as false and uncomfortable.

In this stage the therapist can create alliances with different family members; it depends on the situation and how resistant the family is. Some things to keep in mind when beginning this process: Be honest. Explain the process of therapy to the family, and explain how they might be in for a rough ride.

"Well, I want you to know that we need to work together through some difficulties in your family. This process is going to be uncomfortable, and several times you might want to leave the session. In order to change your system, we need to work on your marriage, we need to create a good team, and put you in charge in your house. Your kids will want to resist, and things might get chaotic for a while, so I need to know if you are both willing to take this. We also need to work on your own issues, your family of origin, your relationship experiences, and your feelings, which are affecting the way you relate to your family and the way it functions. I would like to bring your parents in and resolve any unfinished business you may have with them. These are the issues and dynamics of therapy that I feel are pertinent to our growth. What do you think? Can you take it?"

If the family is resistant and scared to change, this stage will inevitably last longer. Focusing on the positives and giving good feedback will build strength in this family system and encourage them to move forward. In this instance, a therapist might say: "I have a lot of respect for you, I am proud of a family who knows when it is time to ask for help. That is something that only good, caring parents want to do."

This is the time when you need to position yourself as the expert and as part of the family. You need to become on of them; a trusting familiar figure who will transition with the family through good and difficult moments.

Stage 2: Reframing the problem as a family problem. The therapist should reframe the problem as a family problem. It is important for the therapist to de-triangle the IP and help the family understand that these symptoms are part of everyone, and therefore, everyone must share the responsibility. In the case of a couple, the reframe could be related to both of them creating this dysfunction that serves some other purpose; for example,, "Separate to go an take care of your mother," or "to prove your parents right that she was the wrong women for you." "You are creating this scenario to repeat what your parents did."

The therapist can explain that there is a direct link between marital distance, conflict, and these symptoms in their children. Inquiring about their relationship would be appropriate during this stage. Here, the therapist acts as a mediator between the parents and the adolescent. The main question that the therapist would ask everyone is, "What do you need from this family that you are not getting?" In this stage, the therapist can also make contracts between parents and adolescents. When working with Latino, Asian, and African-American client families, it is important to sign a contract with parents and children that gives them structure and guidelines. With these contracts, everyone is compelled to compromise in some kind of change for the benefit of the family as a whole. An example is the following: "Okay, Juan, so you will go to school every day and control your temper. In exchange, your parents will give you more freedom. For instance, you may go to the movies with your friends twice a month." The consequences of noncompliance would be a reduction in allowance and the loss of the telephone privileges, television, and so forth. (This depends on each individual case; every behavior that is expected would be specified, along with the consequences of noncompliance. Parents and child decide, and the therapist monitors the negotiation to help them maintain fairness in their negotiation.) "Mother will stop yelling at Juan and will dedicate more attention to her husband. Dad will curb his drinking, and the couple will stop fighting. Parents will go out for a date twice a month, etc."

The importance of outlining the specifics of the contract is that it will enable the therapist to evaluate the situation, check every week, and assess and link the behaviors of all family members.

With this contract, the therapist is saying to the family: "You all need to change; it is not just Juan's problem, it is the problem of everyone in the family."

For example, the therapist might say: "Why does someone as smart as you need to fail in school? Let's make a deal. I'll help your parents, but you will improve your grades." "Oh, my goodness, it must be such a difficult role to be trapped in the middle of your parents." "When did you make the decision that you were going to protect your mother from your father?" Children are the thermometers of a marriage. If they run a fever, the marriage has a fever, as well. "What would happen if, this time, instead of looking at [his/her] fault, you hold your child and tell [her/him] how much you care about [him/her]?" If a family is very resistant to these attempts, indirect techniques, such as ordeals, paradoxical interventions, and homework assignments are encouraged. In these cases, the therapist will take it personally, declare incompetence, and express feelings of failure.

The therapist may apply Greek chorus (Papp 1980) types of techniques, such as, "My supervisor said I am doing a horrible job, I am failing in my class. What am I doing wrong? Please help me." For example, the therapist can say to the family: "The group thinks that your son is sacrificing his life for the sake of the family. That's why he's misbehaving. But I disagree. I believe you are a great family, and that you're doing the best that you can." Therefore, the family needs to prove to the group that the group's opinion is wrong. With these techniques, the family begins to calm down and take care of the therapist in such a way that family members find it necessary to change their attitude in order to show the therapist that he or she has not failed.

This is a stage when accountability is needed for everyone in the system. It is important for parents and children to understand that only everyone together can make this family more peaceful and content.

Stage 3: De-balancing and Setting Boundaries. This is the most structural stage of therapy. The therapist moves seats, takes the IP from the middle, and sets boundaries around the parental subsystem. The therapist talks about hierarchies, empowers the parents, and teaches communication and parenting skills (Minuchin and Fishman 1981). In this stage, the therapist is very active. He or she can set boundaries, even with his or her own body. In this stage, the therapist makes selective alliances in an attempt to de-balance the system (Minuchin and Fishman). The alliance could be made with the more powerful client, the less powerful one, or the most self-differentiated one. Examples are the following: "I am confused, can one of you tell me who the parent is in this home?" "It seems that, in this house, the mother and father are not on the same page." "It looks as if the mother is married to the IP, and you don't have any place." "When did the IP begin to become the parent in this home?" "When was the last time you had time to be alone without the children?" "When you set a rule and a consequence, you need to stick with them." "Never set a consequence when you are mad." "Try to be calm and not reactive with your son when he argues with you." "Assertiveness is not aggressiveness."

This is one of the stages where resistance becomes stronger. When this happens, the therapist makes statements such as, "I know that this is difficult, a lot of people are afraid of these changes." "I know that it is possible that, next week, you might make excuses for yourself so you don't have to come to therapy." Being direct and challenging are part of the qualities that the therapist should display.

The therapist should continue to explain to the parents that being in charge is the way to go. At this time, the therapist is part of the system and has power and the trust of the family; the therapist should use this power to create situations and challenge parents in such a way that they do not have any other possibility but to take the leadership in the family. The therapist can move parents to anger or emotion by saying things such as, "I wouldn't allow my son to treat me in this way, would you?" "How do you feel when your son yells at you in that way?" "When is it enough for you?"

People need to be prepared for this stage. They need to know that it is difficult and scary. At this point, the therapist needs to intensify the anxiety in order to produce change. In the case of working with a couple, this stage is a very provocative, and an anxiety-producing, confrontational stage. It is the most important moment for couples therapy. It is a challenge and a risk, at this stage, to do something different, to communicate differently, to tolerate anxiety, and to change roles. The therapist needs to be strong and not give in. They will need to fight against homeostasis and be careful of early termination due to extreme fear. At this stage, avoidant conflict and validating couples begin to be more upfront and honest, and volatile couples begin to learn how to talk from their honest feelings instead of getting in constant power struggles. The therapist is the most active, and will do the most coaching, the most mediation, and the most pushing that he or she can do. In general, the therapist is triangulated by the couple taking the place of the IP. This is the time that the therapist needs to play his role in the middle wisely, and strategize in order to help these couples shape their relationship into better form.

Stage 4: Power struggle. It is important to understand that, in this stage, the family begins to struggle with the new changes. There is a tendency to return to past behaviors. The fear of the unknown is very powerful. At this stage, resistance is strong, and the therapist should be assertive and compelled to work again at the joining and the creating-an-alliance stage by building trust with the family at a higher level. This last point is achieved by showing progress and calming tempers. The family members will then notice that the new rearrangement can be more functional and satisfactory for everyone. This is the most difficult stage, where patience and tolerance of frustration should be at the highest level. It is very possible that, at this stage, the family ends the therapy abruptly. Sometimes they leave, but they return later when they feel more prepared, or when the stress becomes once again intolerable.

Some examples of interventions are the following:

Therapist: I know it is hard right now; how frightening it is for the family to do things differently, but in my experience, if you hold on and have faith in the change, you will be very happy afterwards. I can see you are hesitant right now.

Mother: No, I am not.

Therapist: You cancelled the session twice these past two weeks, while previously you were always on time and looked forward to these meetings.

Mother: No, well...

Therapist: Don't worry. This is a normal stage of the process in family therapy. It must be learned. You are a great family, and you're all working very hard to get better. I know you are going to get over this stage, so we can then continue toward achieving your goals.

The message of this stage is: "Don't yield. Calm down. Hold my hand. This is me you're talking to. You know me; we have been working together, and you just need to get over this fear. Put trust in the process."

Stage 5: Emotional stage of intergenerational connection. Goal: beginning of open communication, individuation, and self-definition; and learning how to resolve problems. Family members begin to confront fears, which would lead to increasing their self esteem. This is a nodal moment of the therapy; we are reaching people in their hearts. This is an experience when you show your family who you really are; a stage where people show their vulnerability. They begin to show their love and how important they are to each other. There are moments of hugging and looking into each other's eyes. Is now the time to talk without defenses, with honesty, from the heart?

In order to accomplish these goals, the first thing to do is work with family-of-origin issues. It is about becoming aware of feelings that people have been carrying around, like fear of rejection, abandonment, and feelings of loneliness.

This is achieved through different methods, imaginary guidance, writing letters to parents, role-playing, and the empty-chair technique. Awareness and connection is the ultimate goal of this stage.

This is a stage where Framo's intergenerational approach is mixed with the emotion-eliciting approach of Satir (1972) and Whitaker (1975), so that members of the family can emotionally understand what patterns they are repeating and they can experience the pain that is hidden and projected into the IP. "In this stage, the goal is to create a new therapeutic environment or conversation in which familial interaction is altered to produce a different experience of important family relationships." (Roberto 1991, 454).

In this stage, we invite the parents in. We ask each parent to write a letter to their own parents before they come to the session. You meet with your client and the mother for two hours and your client and the father for two hours, the family together and one hour with each parent alone. Parents read these letters to their adult children, and increase emotional and mental understanding of them and the dynamic in the families, too. This helps the process of change and awareness. An important goal is achieved when adult children see their parents as adults and human beings. This creates empathy and less idealization. In a case where there's resentment, the clients experience the process of forgiving and they can see what patterns they are repeating in their own family. You, the therapist can learn what you are repeating, too, which will help you in the next stage of therapy, "the insight oriented stage". Can you imagine how much information you gather in this way and how much faster it is than seeing only one generation?

After that session you have an exercise between your client and each parent to increase honesty expression of emotions and intimacy (see section that deals with creating intimacy with family members). After that the therapist can do the imaginary guidance exercise with each parent in an individual session with each parent. Finally, the family session where they confront each other and talk about past stories and resolve disagreements and misunderstandings

As always SEFT is customized work, so you have room for modifications depending of the level of flexibility, emotional intelligence, level of openness and level of fear and resistance.

This is amazingly deep, profound and intense work that in my experience creates a lot of modifications in my clients and progress. You may think some clients would not agree to these sessions and bringing the parents in and you would be right - some don't, so I work with what I have. Also, sometimes one person in the marriage agrees to do so and the other doesn't. As an SEFT therapist you are creative and you do the most you can with what you have.

Stage 6: Insight-oriented stage. In the insight-oriented stage, the therapist works with the parents, or with the more differentiated parent. The term "differentiation" refers to emotional maturity that measures the extent to which individuals can think, plan, and follow their own values while being emotionally present with others without reacting to them. They can be close and also have a personal life; they do not give themselves up for fear of losing the people they love. They can make "I" statements (Bowen 1974). Children are not involved in this stage, except for a quick check-in. In this stage the therapist prepares a genogram and teaches some concepts such as triangles, self-differentiation, and coalitions. Some role-playing is performed. The therapist is like a coach (Bowen 1978). The therapist is neutral and remains out of the triangles. The therapist is more concerned about teaching concepts that clients need to process and learn. The therapist focuses on helping the client increase his or her ability to differentiate between feeling and thinking, and to resolve relational problems; parents lower their reactivity and anxiety by focusing more on themselves instead of other people (Bowen 1978).

This is the more intellectual and less reactive stage. If possible, the therapist already has had intergenerational family sessions with different members of the families; this is the preference. Framo (1975) was concerned with bringing the family to the office. He believed that change happened in the session. Each spouse is seen separately and is not present in the partner's sessions. If this is not possible, the therapist should send clients to their families, so that they can experience their family in a different way with all that they have already learned. They can change their position in the family while remaining outside the emotional system; clients become their own coaches to detriangle themselves (Bowen 1978).

However, the therapist makes interpretations, points out similarities in patterns and explains the idea of relating with family members in a non-defensive, non-offensive manner. The main concept to convey is not taking the responses of family members personally. While it is preferable to bring the parents or someone from the family into the session, many times family members are overseas (e.g., Mexico, Vietnam, Cambodia, China, etc.). In those cases, it is recommended that the client bring some family who live in the same town (e.g., a sister, a brother, an aunt). The idea is to be flexible, but to convey to the client that this type of work would be helpful in his or her current life and would link the past with the present. The therapist is a coach and a teacher, and is not so personally involved. He or she prepares families for termination and to be on their own. He or she asks questions, but there are no interpretations. It is important to teach the client to think of emotional moments and challenge cognitions that involve being accepted by everyone or pleasing other people at their own expense. In Latino and Asian culture, this is an especially big issue, because boundaries are sometimes too diffuse, and they affect the nuclear family. In this author's experience from working with Latino families, Latino clients want to set boundaries, feeling that doing so is not being mean or disloyal. It is important to understand that culture will have different rules for emotional maturity. It is essential to understand that cultural differences give a different "flavor" to what constitutes a differentiated person. For instance, daily calls in a Latino family do not necessarily mean being fused or enmeshed; these actions are part of a culture that values a high interpersonal connection (McGoldrick and Carter 2001).

Working in the Asian community would also involve working with people who have been raised to sense that their own self is related to and in harmony with their family, and is also related to a collective self; therefore, in those cases, the concept of differentiation, as defined by Bowen (1974), requires a re-evaluation. The researcher's hypothesis is that it probably should be a compromise between a collective self and an individual self. The level of acculturation would play a significant role in this matter. It is recommended that the therapist work closely with parents and children in order to understand where each of them is coming from.

For example, the therapist can say: "Why are you allowing him to define who you are?" "Why is it so important for you to be accepted by him?" "Nobody makes you feel; you feel." "But why does she have so much power over you? She is a human being, just like you." "You are giving her something that belongs to you. Can you explain to me why you need her acceptance?" "You are not mamma's little girl anymore—you are an adult." "Do you think you can understand that your father was abandoned by his dad? Don't take it personally when he ignores you; he is probably struggling to be a dad and has no role model. It is not about you—it's about him."

In this stage, the client is stronger, and the bond with the therapist is already established. The client is able to accept more, and the therapist helps the client to explore family transmission processes and understand the power of change.

In some cases, the stages overlap. The emotional stage could be the beginning of the treatment, followed by the structural part. With other cases, the therapist needs to begin by being more passive, neutral, and insight-oriented. The therapist needs to explain patterns, to establish the family genogram, and afterwards, to go to the structural stage. The emotional stage is the final one. The therapist needs to be in tune with the family style; at times, this can be complementary, through behaving in the opposite way (i.e., if the family is slow, the therapist will be fast; if the family is too emotional, the therapist will be calm and rational). In other situations, the therapist will find the need to mock the family's style. The therapist's method depends on the family.

It is also important to be on everyone's side and to be in each of the member's shoes. It is important to acknowledge that everyone needs to give something toward resolving the problems in the family. In the case of Latinos, this concept is easy.

It is important to review at this point that, if I can, I already know the parents of my adult clients, and differentiation and resolving past issues is already in process. The client, at this point, is stronger and extremely aware of themselves and the systems where they belong.

Working with Couples:

I do not agree with the theory that, to do couples therapy, both partners must always be present in therapy. I believe couples work involves some individual sessions in order to bring them back together and work on the couple. I also feel strongly about the couple not having individual work with different therapists. Many therapists have many visions, and many visions can complicate resolution.

My secret is a non-secrecy policy; I do not keep secrets. Actually, when I work with avoidant conflict couples, I take advantage of confronting the information they give me while in individual sessions, in order to promote openness and honesty. This helps them to learn how to deal with conflict and issues that are uncomfortable without feeling that they are hurting each other's feelings. Part of the idea of seeing them individually is to understand the concept that a couple is two people, not one, and that the therapist can see how each of them behave when they are alone. I take advantage of these individual sessions when people are too unaware of themselves, or have some personal issues that are affecting the process, or when I begin to observe that, in a session, one person is taking over. I believe individual couples therapy is a process in couples therapy that has helped me obtain the big picture and de-balance the systems that are stuck and full of resistance.

ROLE OF THE THERAPIST

In the beginning stages, the therapist is more involved, active, and strategic, while at the same time, a caring friend and a coach. It is very important that the therapist create a bond with the members of the family; a working alliance where trust evolves. The clients can then accept the pushing and unbalancing techniques that the therapist should apply in order to change the system. The message is that we are all in this together, so let's try to change this together. Later on in the process, the therapist begins to become more neutral, passive, and oriented toward teaching (Bowen 1974). At this point, the therapist is less advice-oriented; the message is that this is your game, not mine. This is your life, not mine. In the beginning stages, the therapist can be involved in triangles and selective alliances, joining with the weakest or the more powerful and de-triangling the client and replacing him or her (Minuchin and Fishman 1981; Minuchin et al. 1996). The pushing is harder when the families are more chaotic and under- functioning. The therapist may use the experience that they have with the clients (feelings such as anger, pity, a need to protect, anxiety, and boredom) as a way to understand what reactions the client produces in different people. The therapist needs to confront clients; generally, there is a need for strong confrontation. Whitaker, Felder, and Whitaker (1965) recommend openly expressing to family members those feelings in order to avoid potential destructive acting out of the feelings. They also recommend being emotionally involved in the family. This concept is conveyed to the client in some way. For example: "When you act like this, I feel you are devaluing me. Is it possible that your son is experiencing the same?" The therapist is a real person in the session; flexible, connected, and creative.

In the later stages, however, the therapist must remain outside of triangles and the family's emotional system (Bowen 1974), because after boundaries and hierarchies have been set and new emotional experiences between family members have been built, the family is stronger and less anxious. As the process of insight and understanding begins, it will help family members gain more control over how to resolve future problems without the need of the therapist.

In the beginning stages of therapy, the therapist gives validation, encouragement, and positive feedback in order to build self-esteem and hope. In later stages, the therapist is less of a cheerleader and more of a neutral, rational, calm presence, because family members become more differentiated as the therapist models for them non-reactivity and the commitment not to overfunction. This change is gradual and responds to the family change. Also, the less needy family members are, the less they need the therapist, and a teaching approach is more convenient and productive for the family.

There are exceptions to this general approach. With certain families, the role of the therapist is initially passive, and toward the end of therapy, more active. An example might be when family members are overly intellectual and mind-focused, using intellectualization as a defensive mechanism; or very rigid, religious families who have difficulties trusting the therapist and present themselves as defensive and detached.

The main point is that the therapist trusts the client's abilities and transmits this trust to the client. The message is, "I believe in you," and this belief must be behind all interventions that the therapist applies. Rogers (1951) would say that therapists provide to the family unconditional, positive regard. For example, "I know you are a smart man, and you know that some of your behaviors need to change for the sake of your family." or "You are a great mother and love your child very much." "I know you can understand that you are repeating patterns, doing what your mother did to you when you were a child, and that hurts you very much; I know you don't want that for your child."

The focus of the therapy is both in the past and the present, in order to create a new future. This model considers that the past and present are interrelated; some understanding of the past helps the present. A new experience with the family of origin, or a new position in the family of origin can provide insight and freedom to present relationships with the wife, the husband, boyfriends, girlfriends, and children. An understanding of the emotional system in the family of origin can provide the client with the freedom to create his or her own style. Understanding the concept of freedom (which includes choices, ideas, and identity) is one of the ultimate goals of therapy, but how do we get there? The answer lies in changing the system, delineating boundaries, experiencing different emotions with family members, learning to communicate openly and clearly, and understanding one's roots. Responsibility for decision-making and ultimate goal-setting is in the hands of each person.

In order to practice SEFT, the therapist must be intuitive, direct, and caring, as well as comfortable with him or herself. Intuition is learned through observation and through connecting and reading others. That is, the therapist should be genuine, real, spontaneous, open, and should exhibit a sense of humor.

Professionalism should be maintained, but in a non-threatening way. This entails joining, becoming part of the family, being cognizant of resistance and comfortable with emotions, and being able to be active and directive in sessions. I truly believe all this requires a therapist who is capable of being fully present.

Other guidelines to follow include being able to remain passive and detached when it is called for, being able to change roles when necessary, and knowing when to do so. We must be honest believers in human resourcefulness. This is not a hat that the therapist puts on; it needs to be part of the therapist's personality, especially , who have a great appreciation and sensitivity for warmth and honesty. The therapist will be aware of his or her core issues and show willingness to work on them, striving for self awareness and growth. The focus of the therapy is in the process; the content is used to read the underlying issues and themes of the family quarrels.

FUNCTIONAL AND DYSFUNCTIONAL FAMILIES

A dysfunctional system is one that is inflexible and lacks communication skills. It is a family where trust, love, warmth, and intimacy are withheld. It may be a family where the couple has no time for themselves, where they neglect one another and lack open communication; a family in which members do not feel free to be themselves and cannot openly ask for what they need. The family may be disconnected or over-involved. These families tend not to be focused on strengths, but rather, are critical of each other. Self-sacrifice and codependent behaviors are dysfunctional (White 1983). While some members may feel secure in their system, others may be tense and scared. Such a family may either lack or have extremely rigid structures and rules. I want you all to remember that "healthy family" does not mean one without conflict.

Whitaker (1976) described healthy families as ones where autonomy does not threaten well-being and satisfaction, and where some degree of commitment exists. In this family, the members are allowed to think and be themselves. A healthy family is a place where members feel safe. Communication is open. When problems arise, they are faced, and solutions are sought. It is a place of warmth and care. Children can grow believing in themselves and can live their life and grow without guilt, by which their families promote growth and the development of self identity. Rules exist and are reinforced, while flexibility and negotiation are present.

Symptoms are due to lack of communication, lack of affection, and lack of respect among family members. Behind the symptoms is the marital conflict that creates over-involvement with children or the neglect of their needs. These are repetitions of dysfunctional generational patterns. Symptoms are like a red flag that one member waves as a way of asking for help for the whole family. It is important not to get caught up with the identified patient's symptom; rather, it is viewed interpersonally as a metaphor for something that is going on in the family. The treatment duration depends on the family and the length of the dysfunction of the symptoms. Symptoms that are entrenched in the family system will take longer to resolve, while new symptoms may only need short-term therapy. For this reason, the therapy is customized or designed specifically for each family. SEFT can range from ten to fifty sessions. From three months to more than year, it depends on the capacity and the standards that the family or individuals have for growing, and how long they can take the pushing. Often, families have the tendency to leave if they reach their limitations, but in general, they return if problems arise.

Techniques used include specific strategies, provocative questions, enactments, pushing, confrontation interpretations that create awareness of patterns that have been repeated over time, lowering reactivity, debalancing selective alliances, gestalt exercises, and de-triangling. But what does strategy mean? It means having a goal, and one must find a way to achieve that goal without the involved parties having insight of your procedure. However, it is very important letting your clients know once the procedure over. Because this model is about integrity and accountability, I believe strategies do not break that standard, due to the fact that our first commitment to our clients is to do whatever it takes to help them achieve their goal.

SEFT incorporates several important strategies: (a) the role-modeling strategy. Within role-modeling, I use two techniques: (1) the broker technique; and (2) the validating technique. It is important to mention that, during therapy, music is used to create emotional moments. Imaginary guidance and eye contact are used in combination with music to promote closeness and intimacy.

Role modeling strategy (Bandura 1969): The therapist assumes the role of one parent and shows a problem-solving skill and a new way of communicating. In other words, the therapist steps in to model for the parent. The goal of this strategy is to break resistance through modeling, instead of directly instructing.

This can be explicit, for example:

Therapist: If Juan were my child, I would have said to him…

Or direct assumption of the role without explanation, for example, saying to the IP:

Therapist: So you did not follow your part of the contract, now you lost the privilege of using the phone, as arranged in the contract.

IP: Who are you? You are not my mother.

Therapist: You are right, but your parents came to me for help, I am doing my job.

Mother: I'm telling you, I am your mother, and your privilege of phone use is out for the week, end of discussion.

Therapist: Very good, Mom. I can see how much you care about your daughter.

IP: [Crying] I hate you.

Therapist: I know you feel frustrated right know, but you are a smart girl you understand that contracts are to be followed.

Broker technique: The therapist assumes a middle stand where everybody is entitled to a perspective, and negotiation is promoted. The goal here is to teach families about negotiation, so in the future they can apply this without the help of a therapist.

Case example:

IP: I can never invite friends over my house.

Parent: Because I don't trust you; you are always in trouble.

IP: You see? He never listens to me.

Therapist: Grandpa, do you think you can trust Saul? [To the parent] What do you want in exchange?

Parent: I want Saul to clean his room and check in and out.

Therapist: Okay, Saul, do you think you can do that?

IP: Yes I can.

Therapist: So let's make a deal in writing. I will check every week to see how we are all doing.

Validating technique: The therapist looks into the client's eyes and transmits messages of hope and trust. The goal here is to provoke the parent's jealousy and show how someone could give their child unconditional love. This technique is basic to this model; validation is a powerful tool when working with Latino, Asian, and African-American populations. It is important to be aware of these cultural traits, because these cultures focus more on the negative to encourage improvement. Meanwhile, in the U.S., parents use a lot more positive reinforcement.
Case example:

IP: I have so many doubts. I think my mother is right; I'm not going to succeed.

Therapist: I know you are going to succeed. I've had a lot of clients like you, and they are very successful. Right now, I want you to look into my eyes and believe me when I say you are going to make it.

IP: [Crying] It is so nice to listen to someone saying that.

Mother: I'm sorry if I said that to you, my mother used to say that too, and it really hurts. [Mother stands up and hugs client.]

Mother: You are wonderful. I love you. [Both cry.]

These following techniques are useful in promoting the outpouring of feelings in which the client is coaxed into words venting emotions.

Bad Guy and Good Guy Strategy: This strategy can be used two ways. One way would be letting your client know that your supervisor feels that you are not doing a good job. You explain to your client your feelings of desperation and fear of, perhaps, not passing the class. The goal with this strategy is to have your client begin wanting to protect you. This protection will create an alliance between you and your client, which would prove your supervisor wrong and facilitate change within your client. The second way this strategy works, when you explain your client that your supervisor has no faith in him or her to change and you had to stand up and fight for your client's ability to improve. You would express how much you believe in his or her abilities. The goal of this strategy is to empower your client indirectly. It works with clients who are week, have low self-esteem, and have difficulty with leadership.

The Power of Sacrifice Strategy: You rephrase the system as a way where the client seems to be sacrificing him or herself for someone who they dislike. Due to the negative feelings they have for this person, clients will try to prove you wrong, and that will create in them an empowerment to change the symptom.

The Failure Strategy I: Here you declare to your client that you are failing them and admit that their lack of improvement is your fault. The goal with this strategy is to help clients to acknowledge and see positives. Clients who are very negative and pessimistic begin to improve with this strategy.

STRATEGIES SPECIFICALLY TAILORED TO COUPLES AND FAMILIES

Selective Alliance Strategy: In the distancer-pursuer relationship, the therapist shall build an alliance with the pursuer. Example: The partner who pursues the other to have sex all the time shall agree to a contract that they will not approach their partner for sex for one week. Other examples: nagging and calling all the time.

When working with families, the therapist should create that alliance with the most motivated member of the family. For example, in a case of a family where the mother is very unreliable but the daughter is the opposite, the therapist would talk to the daughter alone and explain that they will play a game in session where she will have to challenge her mother in front of the therapist. As the daughter is challenging the mother, the therapist will challenge the daughter and defend the mother. The goal is for the mother to commit to change and become oppositional to her daughter, through which she will prove her daughter wrong and create an alliance with the therapist.

Empowering Strategy: The therapist takes sides with the couple, through which he or she will create an alliance with the oppressed partner. For example: in a case with a couple where the husband does not treat his wife well, and they are in the process of divorce, the therapist begins to express how lucky the husband is to have a wife as nice as she is. The therapist would hint at the idea that similar clients would not be as nice and understanding as his wife, and would emphasize how these clients are impressed with his wife's behavior. The goal of this strategy is to suggest indirectly to the disempowered partner to stand up for his or herself.

Extremity Strategy: The idea behind is to exaggerate the consequences of a particular situation. For example: in a case of a couple who fights all the time while the children are witnessing their struggles, the therapist could warn the parents about the possible extreme consequences these fights can have on their children. Giving examples of extreme cases in the past also can heighten the consequences.

Failure Strategy II: The therapist will declare extreme sadness and hopelessness about the couple's or the family's situation and admit that he feels he has failed in his work. This strategy is all about emotions and feelings of hurt, because as a therapist, you could not help the family. In session, you can criticize yourself in front of the client about why you did not succeed. The client will rush to your help and will try to defend you from yourself. In this process, the couple or family will suggest ways that you can help them.

Commitment Strategy: Ask the client to describe their level of commitment from "1-10." If the client responds with a number less than seven, you must challenge their commitment. If the client responds with a higher number, but you feel their actions do not reflect that number, than you need to challenge them again.

SPECIFIC TECHNIQUES FOR TEENAGERS

Hate Versus Attention Strategy: When a teenager express hate towards parents in session, you will reframe that hate as the teenager's need for attention. For example: in a case where the mother is always being told that she is hated by her daughter, you can reframe that as her daughter's wish to spend more time with her. You can recommend to the mother that she might attend class with the teenager. Since this would be rather shameful for the daughter, this is the time to negotiate the improvement of the behavior.

If You Hate Me Just Change Strategy: In a case where the teenage client does not like the therapist, the therapist can advise the client to change for the better, otherwise therapy might last forever. This can mean that the client will have to attend these sessions longer and the teenager will be driven to change, because he or she will not want to continue therapy.

The next chapter will introduce you to experiential exercises with individuals.

EMOTIONAL EXERCISES

IMAGINARY GUIDANCE:

"Letting go of the pain from the past can create a new, healing future."
Dr. Liliana Cabouli

THIS IS FOR ADULTS AND TEENAGERS ONLY. IT IS TO BE PERFORMED WITH INDIVIDUAL CLIENTS ONLY.

TO BEGIN:

The first step is to guide the person to a deep relaxation stage. For this technique, you might consider putting on some relaxing music and guiding the client to take deep breaths; inhaling and exhaling. At this point, you would begin to work through the body, asking the client to relax each and every part of his or her body. By asking to take one last deep breath the client should be experiencing a very heavy sensation in their body, creating an ultimate sense of relaxation. During this entire exercise, the therapist wants to be conscious of their tone of voice, trying to maintain a very gentle and soothing tone.

THE LETTING-GO EXERCISE:

AFTER RELAXATION:

I want you to turn your mind on like a screen. I want you to go to your house when you were a child; return to your past. I want you to create a time when you were five, six, seven, or eight years old (specify the age in correlation with the abuse, or a situation that was painful). Remember the sights, sounds, and smells of your childhood. Look around you and remember the setting--your house or apartment where you lived. Picture the sights of the neighborhood—the people living there, the children playing there, the landscape growing there, the sky, and the weather. Listen to the sounds of the animals, the sounds of the cars, children, parents, friends, and games. Remember the smell of winter, spring, summer, and fall. As you approach the front door of your home, give permission to yourself to experience all your senses—your thoughts, your feelings, your sense of touch, taste, smell, and sound. Let your intuition and feelings accompany you as your guide. Picture the entrance of your home—the walkway, the door, the windows, the doorbell. Open the door and enter your childhood home. What do you see? What do you feel? Who do you see? Remember the place where you used to play, eat, watch TV, and where you used to sleep. Look at your room and see yourself as a child. Through the eyes of the child inside you, look at your bed where you slept, the toys that you played with and the clothes that you wore. Look at the eyes of your child. Remember how you felt. Were you happy? Were you unhappy? Did you feel like nobody was there for you? Were you sad or lonely? Did you feel safe or unprotected? Connect with those feelings that your child feels. Be honest. Be aware if your child is in pain. Don't be afraid to face it. Experience these feelings of your child. Hug your child. Hold your child and give your child unconditional love, and tell your child everything is going to be all right. Everything is going to be okay. Feel the relief that the child is feeling. The child can relax, because everything is being taken care of. The child knows there is no need to worry anymore, because everything is being taken care of. Let all the fear and worry melt away. That little child is secure and happy, and you can let the child go.

Now you see your mother entering your room. Look into the eyes of your mom. How is she feeling? Does she feel guilty? Is she rejecting you? Is she caring? Is she distant? How were you feeling when you were growing up? Was she there for you when you were growing up, or not? I want you to tell your mom everything you wanted to tell her, but never did. What is her response to you? I want you to forgive her if she hurt you, or to thank her if she was there for you. Enjoy this moment of connection with your mother as she is there for you and available to you. Now you are ready to let her go, and so she leaves the room.

Now you see your father entering your room. Look into the eyes of your dad. How is he feeling? Does he feel guilty? Is he rejecting you? Is he caring? Is he distant? How were you feeling when you were growing up? Was he there for you when you were growing up or not? I want you to tell your dad everything you wanted to tell him, but never did. What is his response to you? I want you to forgive him if he hurt you or thank him if he was there for you. Enjoy this moment of connection with your father as he is there for you and available to you. Now you are ready to let him go and so he leaves the room.

Now you are going to leave the house leaving behind all those feelings of pain, abandonment, loneliness, anguish, sadness, and anger. Now you are feeling peaceful, happy, and a sense of relief. Now you are going to go to a beautiful, peaceful place—a long spacious beach. You will see sky spackled with silky, white, billowing clouds, surrounded by fleshy, layered, pastel-colored mountains with a slight cool breeze gently caressing your face and body. Take a deep breath of the sweet, fresh ocean air and feel it surge through your body, cleansing your soul as you exhale, letting go of all those heavy feelings. You continue walking and come across black balloons anchored in the sand, each representing the feelings of loneliness, hopelessness, worthlessness, inadequacy, failure, despair, anguish, worry, pain, anger, abuse, misery, and neglect. With all your might and strength, you pull and dislodge each balloon until no more balloons remain—releasing each negative feeling, one at a time, as you watch those dark, negative feelings fly away and disappear in the clouds. You are now at peace. (You customize this for each client)

Using letters to emphasize the emotional connection:

For some clients, you might ask them to write a letter to the person they really need to speak with: mother, father, abuser, ex-husband, etc. The exercise consists in first doing relaxation, imaginary guidance to their childhood house, or to a nice, relaxing environment. When the client is in that place, you ask them to see, for example, their mother coming, and you coach the client to look into their mother's eyes. Then you say, "I am going to read your letter you wrote to your mother, and I want you to imagine that you are saying this to her." The therapist will read it softly, slowly, and deeply, to promote the presence of emotions. After mother, you go to their father and the other people you have a letter for, and repeat the same process.

When finished, you will coach them to see in front of them an intense light. At the end of it, all the people the client loves are there; for example, husband and kids. You would say that the light is the light of self-awareness and enlightenment; it is the light of growth and honesty and intimacy. "When you made the decision that you want to transcend the light, you knew that there were going to be obstacles and difficult moments, but also growth and happiness. After this transcendence, you will be more available for your family and people you love, because you will forgive and heal past the pain." It is ultimately the decision of the client if they want to transcend or not. The therapist is only there to offer their hand to guide you through the walk.

When you do family of origin work and bring parents in, you ask them also to write letters to their parents. In the session, they read them in front of their adult children as a way to create in them some understanding of the parents and what they went through. In general, there is a lot of repetition in multigenerational transmission process (Bowen) and it increases awareness, intimacy and closeness with those parents.

EXPERIENTIAL EXERCISES FOR COUPLES.

Intimacy is to love what freedom is to human nature.
Dr. Liliana Cabouli

TECHNIQUES FOR COUPLES THERAPY
1) Fear of intimacy desensitization

INSTRUCTION:
I WANT YOU BOTH TO LOOK INTO EACH OTHERS' EYES, MAINTAINING EYE CONTACT AND THIS LEVEL OF INTIMACY.

Directive:

"I am going to start a phrase and you are going to complete it. First partner A and then partner B."

What hurts me the most about our relationship is…

What I need from you is…

What I am willing to compromise in this relationship to make it work is…

What I did to contribute to what is going on right now is…

Strategic Experiential Family Therapy

What I like about you the most is…

What I find difficult to understand about you is…

What I feel with you is…

What I want you to know is…

What I fear the most is…

I want to tell you that…

In this relationship, I commit to…

I want you to know that, while I was growing up, I thought I was…

As a little [boy/girl], I use to feel…

In my family, as a whole, I felt…

In school, I felt…

With my mother, I felt….

With my father, I felt…

With my brothers and sisters, I felt…

What I always was wanting from my parents was…

What I wouldn't want to feel anymore in my life is…

My most terrible fear is…

[Therapist should try to create an ambiance of intimacy by being soft and firm.]

INSTRUCTION

"I WANT YOU TO HOLD EACH OTHER'S HANDS, REMAINING SILENT AS YOU LOOK INTO EACH OTHERS EYES WHILE I PLAY THIS MUSIC. [For example, "Do You Know" by Diana Ross] I WANT BOTH OF YOU

TO GIVE EACH OTHER A HUG, AND I WANT YOU TO RELAX IN THIS ENCOUNTER. [Play relaxation music].

Guide them to relax and feel connected with a relaxation exercise. You could say something like, "I want both of you to feel every part of your partner's body in full contact and to face each other by putting your arms around your partners. Open yourself to this encounter by relaxing and feeling your love for each other. You are close to this person. There is a love that exists between you, the one you share so many moments with; the one with whom you have children with. Connect in this encounter."
You need to make the story specific each individual couple.

Imaginary guidance couple work. You will induce relaxation, as you do individually, but both of them will be holding hands.
You need to start again by walking through each part of their bodies, continuing with the relaxation. When they are both relaxed, you will talk to them about everything that they experience together; when they first met, when they first kissed, made love, married, and had their first child. At the time you begin to do this type of work, you need to have the history of this couple, and with this information, you will create a custom made imaginary guidance for them.

SHOWING VULNERABILITY

*There is no intimacy without showing vulnerability
Being vulnerable in-front of someone is
an act of strength, and true love.*
Dr.Liliana Cabouli

INSTRUCTION:

HAVE BOTH PARTNERS STAND. PARTNER A WILL FACE THE BACKSIDE OF PARTNER B, WHILE PARTNER A SAYS THE FOLLOWING:

I always thought that if I told you...you would reject me.
My biggest secret is…
I believe that the worst part of me is…
I feel inadequate when…
I fear you would abandon me if…
What I cannot accept about me is…
What I wish I could change is…
If you die tomorrow, I would regret…
I feel lonely with you when…
How I differ from you is...
I always disagree with you about…
What I enjoy doing the most in life is…
I feel disappointed when you…
What I dislike most about you is…

What I would change about you if I could is…
What I feel is missing from this relationship is…
What I need to give up to be with you is…
What I feel difficult to put up with in
   order to be with you is…
What I'm not willing to compromise to
   be in this relationship is…
The values that I share with you are…
What I like you the most about you is…
What I would never want you to change is…
What I love about our relationship is…
What I love the most about you is…
What I am willing to compromise in our relationship is…

My question is: can you accept me the way I am?

AT THIS POINT, HAVE PARTNER B TURN AROUND TO FACE PARTNER A AND DISTANCE HIM OR HERSELF FROM PARTNER A BY HAVING PARTNER B TAKE FIVE STEPS BACK AWAY FROM PARTNER A. NOW HAVE PARTNER A REPEAT THE LAST STATEMENT IN A LOUD VOICE, AND HAVE PARTNER B ANSWER "YES" OR "NO," WITH NO "BUTS" [This is to show the level of intimacy the partners are having.] IF THE ANSWER IS YES, HAVE PARTNER A TAKE ONE STEP CLOSER TO PARTNER B. PARTNER A WILL REPEAT THE QUESTION FOUR TIMES, ASKING IN A SOFTER AND SOFTER VOICE AS THEY APPROACH THE ACCEPTING PARTNER B UNTIL THEY ARE STANDING FACE TO FACE AT WHICH POINT THE THERAPIST WILL PLAY MUSIC. IF THE RESPONSE IS NO, THEN PARTNER A WILL STEP BACK AWAY FROM PARTNER B, WHILE REPEATING THE QUESTION FOUR

TIMES AND STEPPING BACKWARD OR FORWARD ACCORDING TO THE RESPONSE GIVEN.

NOW HAVE PARTNER B COMPLETE THE STATEMENTS, FOLLOWING THE SAME STEPS OF THE EXERCISE.

Honesty is the baseline of a deep relationship
Honesty is a gift of love
Honesty is an act of caring
Dr. Liliana Cabouli

Open communication exercise

Sometimes we can love without trust but it hurts.
Dr. Liliana Cabouli

BUILDING TRUST

My trust level with you is low, medium, or high.
I felt betrayed by you when…
What I need to happen in our relationship to trust more is…
The meaning of trust for me is…
My feelings from my family of origin about trust is…
When I need you I [trust/don't] trust that you will be there for me…
I can rely on you for…
I can't rely on you for…
What makes me trust you is…
My question is, can I trust you?

REPEAT EXERCISE ABOVE, BUT THIS TIME WITH THE OPTIONAL RESPONSE, EITHER: "YES, YOU CAN TRUST ME. I'LL BE THERE FOR YOU," OR "NO, YOU CANNOT TRUST ME. I DON'T KNOW IF I CAN BE THERE FOR YOU." ASK PARTNER A IF THEY BELIEVE WHAT THEIR PARTNER IS SAYING IS TRUE. IF YOU DON'T BELIEVE WHAT YOUR PARTNER IS SAYING, HAVE THEM TELL PARTNER B, "I'M SORRY I DON'T BELIEVE YOU, AND I DON'T TRUST YOU." HAVE PARTNER A TAKE ONE STEP BACK. THE THERAPIST NEEDS TO ADDRESS THE DISTANCE AS THE DISTANCE OF INTIMACY AND TRUST THAT THEY NEED TO WORK ON IN ORDER TO SUCCEED IN THEIR MARRIAGE.

FORGIVING, NOT FORGETTING INFIDELITY

GIVE THESE QUESTIONS TO THE PERSON WHO WAS CHEATED ON AND ASK HIM OR HER TO CHOOSE WHICH OF THESE QUESTIONS SHE WANTS HIM OR HER TO RESPOND TO.

> When I realized that you cheat on me I felt…
> Why did you cheat on me?
> In what way are we going to avoid this happening again?
> How would you feel if I cheated on you?
> What were you feeling when you cheated on me?
> The only way I would overcome this is if…
> My trust level with you is…
> If you love me, why did you cheat on me?
> Would you forgive me if I cheated on you?

THE CHEATER AFTERWARD WILL ANSWER THOSE QUESTIONS ONE ON ONE. AFTER THAT, THE CHEATER WILL ASK:

Why did you decide to forgive me?
What do you think was missing from our relationship?
How does the fact that I was disloyal to you feel?
Do you really think that you can forgive me?
Why do you think that I cheated on you?
What needs to change to build more trust with you?

AFTER THEY FINISH, THE THERAPIST COACHES THEM TO LOOK INTO EACH OTHERS EYES AND WILL PUT SOME MUSIC ON AND LET THEM LOOK AT EACH OTHER DURING THE DURATION OF THE SONG.

CREATING INTIMACY BETWEEN FAMILY MEMBERS

PARTNER A AND B STAND UP AND LOOK INTO EACH OTHERS' EYES.

> [Mom/Dad], I want you to know how I felt when I was growing up.
> The question I always wanted to ask you is…
> How I want this relationship to be different is…
> I've always been afraid to tell you …
> What I want you to know about me is..
> My experience of you when I'm around you is…
> The way I see you is…
> What I want you to appreciate about me is…
> [I felt/I didn't feel] accepted by you…
> Your love is [conditional/unconditional]…
> What I always needed from you is…
> If I could change one thing about the way we relate, it would be…
> What I want you to accept about me is…
> What I hope we can have is…
> The best thing you give to me is…
> What I hope our relationship will look like is…
> The thing I like the most about our relationship is…

What I like the most about you is...
The way I saw our family was...
The way I see the family is
Our communication is...
My trust level with you is...

I WANT BOTH OF YOU TO HUG EACH OTHER AND FEEL CONNECTED FROM A PLACE OF ACCEPTANCE AND LOVE. I WANT YOU TO LOOK AT EACH OTHER'S EYES AND THEN PLAY MUSIC.

MOM, I WANT YOU TO REMEMBER WHEN YOUR [DAUGHTER/SON] WAS BORN AND ALL THE HOPES AND DREAMS YOU HAD FOR YOUR LITTLE BABY; THE FIRST STEPS, THE FIRST WORDS, THE FIRST DAY OF SCHOOL, ETC.

I WANT YOU TO FEEL CONNECTED WITH YOUR [DAUGHTER/SON] AND FEEL THIS MOMENT OF CLOSENESS AND INTIMACY.

Part of the deal of this particular style of therapy is that the therapist should be able to feel comfortable with confronting and pushing the client out of their comfort zone in order to create awareness and a new emotional experience.

The Decision Making Process:

There are some points where there is no other thing left to do than to plant both feet on the ground and stand up. There is a crucial time when the couple needs to set boundaries and renegotiate in terms of something acceptable for each partner. In those cases the therapist needs to promote clarity to the situation by framing.

> Therapist to husband: You said that you are scared of your wife, and that she is non-negotiable, that you yield a lot, that you are trying to give her love in the way that you learn and can, even though you know that she is asking for something different than what you are giving. She is asking for love and connection, instead of presents and material objects.

> Therapist to wife: On one hand, you said that you feel rejected and lonely while with him, and hurt because he does not deliver what you need. He does not touch you or give you eye contact. You said you feel unloved in this relationship; you said that you feel unhappy and tired of waiting for him to open up and to be there with you and for you. You are even willing to end the relationship if this does not happen. However, on the other hand, you said that you are not willing to give up the relationship. I don't see a lot of room here for many decisions, do you?

> Husband to Wife: But you don't want to change.

> Therapist: So what are you going to do about it?

> Wife to Husband: You are right I don't want to change.

> Therapist to Husband: It sounds like you have only two choices here, am I right?

> Husband to Wife: It is always your way or the highway.

Therapist: Well, you can choose not to accept those conditions, can't you?

Wife to Husband: Told you.

Husband to Wife: I feel threatened by you.

Wife to Husband: That is not my issue, it is yours.

Therapist to Husband: Well, as I told you, I don't see a lot of room for negotiation. Your wife is being clear where she stands. What about you, where do you stand?

Husband to Therapist: I love my wife, and I am willing to compromise.

Therapist: Are you okay with this decision?

Wife and Husband: Yes.

Therapist: Let's try to see if either of you understand what choices you have made in this deal.

The bottom line is that the therapist should be able to think clearly in moments of tension, and he or she is able to keep the ball in the court of the couple.

Couples therapy:

Couples therapy goes through the same stages of family or individual therapy, but includes the themes of sex and dating. I find a lot of couples that don't have sex or don't date. As a therapist, you need to address these issues and frame them as a way to take care of the relationship and not take it for granted.

The phrase is "A good family is based in a good marriage, which is a great example for your kids". This is the moment where the concept of a safe haven sounds risky to me, because in my experience women who feel unattended by their husbands threaten to divorce them and only then the men react by getting in the begging mood of wanting to resolve the marriage. I have a lot (70%) of my clients who are at this stage in their relationship and it's mostly the men who are the ones that call for the appointment, after the wives threaten them to leave them.

Sex is also an important topic of which I talk openly. I find a lot of women not enjoying their sex life due to resentment and lack of intimacy. The main goal of couples therapy is to increase intimacy between partners. You do exercises with them (see section on intimacy desensitization).You do imaginary guidance with each partner and you help to promote and create an environment of openness and honesty. This is the main goal, so each can express openly their needs and can be themselves in the relationship. The concept of commitment and integrity is proposed .

Individual Therapy Incorporated within Couples Work

When treating couples, I propose that it may not always be in the best interest of the couple to treat them as a couple, and that in some cases it may be more productive to treat the partners individually. For example, couples who have problems with avoiding conflict may initially benefit more from individual treatment to overcome their fear of hurting the other partner, and to be able to confront their partner without feeling guilty.

I also question the effectiveness of having three separate therapists; one for the couple itself, and one for each partner. Because therapists often have different treatment styles and recommendations, a couple could become more confused and the possibility of creating mixed messages can occur. So if you work with a couple, I propose that only one therapist work with the couple as a unit and both partners individually. If the money is not an issue I would recommend co-therapy. A NON-SECRECY POLICY is important. This allows the therapist to manipulate the system, especially when the couple is extremely resistant. Here is an example of a contract that you can have your clients sign.

"Due to the fact that couples therapy will involve some individual interviews, the therapist will not keep secrets between partners and family members. The reason for this is that such secrets can affect the treatment and the position of the therapist with the couple. In extreme circumstances, the therapist might consider that certain information shall not be told, but that would be left to the discretion of the therapist."

At the start of a couple's therapy, you need to be part of the system in order to de-balance and create selective alliances and change the unproductive cycle. For example, you can advise a couple in which the husband calls all the time to stop calling, without telling the wife. This throws off the cycle of behavior and enables them to grow.

In some cases when they are not willing to address a lot of issues, the therapist, with a non-secrecy policy will see both individually and then as a couple and share some of the information as a way to brake the ice, or confront them when they are not honest.

I have found that couples who are stuck have three different ways of approaching problems: non-confrontation, non-acknowledgment of them, or fighting with no resolution.

Non-Confrontational Couples

A non-confrontational couple is a couple that resolves problems without actually resolving the problem. A non-confrontational person might minimize the problem and decide that it's not worth the inevitable conflict or disagreement. The non-confrontational person fears that, "If I hurt you then you will hurt me," and he or she can not deal with that.

Case example:

Therapist: You are telling her that your sexual life is great with her, but you told me that you feel that she is disconnected from you, and that hurts.

Husband: Well, that is right. I mean, I do have some concerns.

Therapist: You ask me to help this relationship to grow; one of the things this relationship needs is honesty and addressing issues to be resolved. I am sure your wife would be delighted to hear what you have to say. Am I right?

Wife: Yes, I am

Therapist: Would you feel devastated if he is honest?

Wife: Not at all

Husband: I feel that you don't participate in bed with me; you are not with me.

Wife: [Getting defensive]: Well, what do you want me to do???

Therapist: Okay, I see that you are getting defensive. If you do that, you are sending a message that you can't take the honesty from your husband; therefore, this tension between you and him will continue. What do you want to do?

Wife: Okay, I am sorry; in what way can I be with you?

Husband: I would like you to kiss me more, look at me when we make love, and be more active.

Therapist: What a gift of love, being so honest.

Wife: Okay, let's try to work on that.

COUPLES THAT AGREE AND VALIDATE

Validating people don't want to be abandoned, rejected, or ignored, so they express understanding and unconditional acceptance. They even might not react or feel much when criticized, because they are disconnected from their own feelings, as well as those of others. For them, it's easier to avoid the emotions connected with the problem, and it's easier to agree than to disagree and risk the other person abandoning, rejecting, or confronting. Validating people are people-pleasers who care about image, and they often will say, "I understand." They give what the other person wants. With both avoidant and validating couples, you need to draw out the conflict by creating a selective alliance with one of the partners who is more willing to open up and address conflict. This can be done by meeting with each individually and pushing one partner to confront the other one. Anticipating the fact that the confronted partner will resist, prepare the other partner with questions like: "What are you going to do when your partner decides not to come to therapy anymore?" "Are you going to support me confronting him/her?"

>Husband: I cheat on you, and I'm so angry at myself.
>
>Wife: I understand. I'm sorry you're hurt. I'm worried that you will do this again.
>
>Husband: I know. I made a big mistake letting someone in.
>
>Wife: I'm sorry you're hurt. It's difficult for me to see you so hurt.
>
>Therapist: I see that you have a lot of understanding about each other, and you care about each other

so much. Even how well you communicate surprises me so much, but I am also surprised that the outcome of this relationship was cheating.

Husband: You are the most amazing, beautiful, sexy woman in my life, and I'm so lucky to have you.

Wife: Yes, there are so many good things about our family, and I don't understand why you cheat on me.

Therapist: Are you trying to say that you're not buying his compliments?

Wife: Well, yes, I don't think it's realistic what he's saying, but I know he loves me.

Therapist: I continue seeing that you have a lot of understanding with each other, and it seems to me that you don't have any problems with this marriage.

Wife: Well, he cheats on me.

Therapist: But you know he loves you.

Husband: Yes, I do. I need more sex.

Wife: I understand that, but I can't be all that you want. I can't have sex three times a day. And if you need that, you're probably going to cheat on me again, and I'm worried that I can't fulfill you.

Therapist: Do you feel that it's your responsibility to meet all his needs at the expense of your own needs?

Wife: He's going to abandon me or cheat on me if I don't fulfill his sexual needs.

Husband: I don't want to lose you.

Therapist: I don't know the solution for your problem, because there seems to be a lot of understanding and sacrificing. So I see you have two choices: to "fuck" twenty-four hours a day, or to cheat whenever. I suppose those could be reasonable choices for you. I don't know that I could be the right therapist for you, because I don't know that I could be as understanding as you two. If my husband cheated on me, I would be pissed off. [To the wife] I admire you so much that you could be so understanding of your husband.

Wife: I *am* pissed off!

Therapist: Oh, I didn't realize that. You're very good at faking it.

Wife: I am pissed and hurt. How could you do that to me?

Husband: I hate myself for that.

Therapist: In what way does that hate help you? I do not experience you as connected in this therapy, and in order to make this work, we need to be a team, and you need to be involved, and I don't see you doing that. I experience your words as empty.

Wife: You know what? I agree. You always tell me I'm so wonderful, but if I'm so wonderful, why do you cheat on me?

THE ARGUMENTATIVE COUPLE

Argumentative couples have issues with anger control, and they have difficulties with negotiating or resolving problems. Such couples have the tendency to present dilemmas that have no solutions. These couples are most likely incompatible, and they do not have much in common, however they stayed together, and in constant power struggles. Their relationship can be described as a rollercoaster ride; where they hope the therapist will point out the right person versus the wrong person. In general, these couples are emotionally enmeshed, and one of them will want to leave the relationship while the other struggles to save it. The process of therapy with such couples tends to last longer, and it involves hard work. The goal is to lessen the fights and teach them to appreciate their good times and to understand and accept each other. One of the major goals is to teach them to compromise, if they want to continue to be with each other.

As a therapist, be aware of possible feelings of frustration, because that is related to the up and downs of such relationships. It is encouraged to create a very strong alliance with both partners by validating their feelings continually.

SEFT is an extremely appropriate model for these type of couples.

Case example:

Husband: You should find a job.

Wife: Don't you understand I have five kids? It will cost me more money to hire a babysitter than to be in the house.

Husband: I don't want to spend more money than I am spending right now.

Wife: Don't you understand what a marriage is? We love each other, have great sex, have fun together, but I cannot take it anymore that you are cheap. I am really thinking of leaving this relationship.

Husband: Okay, if that is what you really want, then I will just leave the relationship.

Wife: Do what you need to do.
[Husband leaves the room but comes back two seconds later.]

Husband: I don't understand you, we love each other.

Therapist: [Needs to explain what the couple does.] This is what I am seeing here: you have an issue, you begin to discuss it, you both become inflexible. Then you feel like staying together is breaking your own integrity. At this point, you make the decision to leave the relationship, then [to the husband] you leave the room, then you come back. It looks like, in order to solve an issue, you need to get into extremes. Unfortunately, this is a cycle that escalates and repeats itself. In the long run, it will hurt your relationship and create anger, and the pain and disappointment will cover up the areas of love and passion that you have right now. If you want to resolve this marriage, we have to find a different way to solve problems. It won't be an easy job.

Therapies have different moments when different members of the family are the protagonists: the IP stage, the mother stage, the father stage, the older-brother stage, the middle-sister stage, and so on. Everyone has his or her own moments—thus, there is the realization that there are no members in the family who are more or less important. Everyone is just as important. The underlying message is, "This is nobody's problem in particular; this is everyone's problem."

CULTURE AND THERAPY

*What Counselors Need to Understand about
How to Work with Other Cultures.*

What is cultural diversity, and does it really matter? Published in AAMFT quarterly magazine, 2005.

Is culture a concept you can learn, or is culture something you can only learn by experience? What concerns me is that, despite my status as a Spanish-speaking, Latin-American female therapist, I was never consulted for my cultural perspective in my profession by colleagues who were treating Spanish speaking clients. It caught my attention because when working in different agencies at which 50 percent of the clientele were Hispanic, and being the only one with that background, I was never approached with any question about culture. I came to this country eight years ago, with no knowledge of English, thinking that, because of my training in Argentina, my experience and coursework would count for something. Instead, I found out that I was going to have to get a doctorate in order to practice in the same capacity as I had in Argentina. That was scary enough, but when I started the program, I was even more alarmed by the unfriendliness and coldness of the classmates. I felt completely unwelcome in a way I never experienced before. No one said hello, no one asked me where I came from, no one showed interest, and yet this was a class of aspiring therapists. The irony was that the class I was taking was "Ethnicity and Culture," and the professor was half-Asian and was explaining to the students how they should accept and embrace cultural differences. I was observing a room full of staring, disinterested, silent, passive, unengaged students who responded as if the professor was speaking another language.

At this point, I realized that I was in trouble, and that it was going to be very difficult to feel accepted and welcomed. I felt that I might always be regarded as an outsider. That experience, for which words can do no justice, was very painful. I felt as if everything that had meaning and value didn't apply here. I felt that I had to start my life all over again and prove and justify my existence. In this process, I had to relearn all the rules and I experienced a lot of misunderstanding and conflicts and rejection. I had to constantly explain myself and ask questions repeatedly, because I couldn't understand. I remember working at St. Vincent De Paul and meeting this counselor, who said to me, "Well, some people might think you're stupid because you have an accent, and I want to apologize for those people who don't know how to make a foreigner feel welcome." I thought to myself, "Oh my gosh, the fact that I speak two languages doesn't count? People could still perceive me as stupid. I couldn't believe it. It was the first time I received such feedback. I never forgot that statement. Imagine that your whole life, you thought of yourself as intelligent and smart, and then you go to another country and they think that you are stupid. The bottom line is that I did not experience a lot of people being curious about my culture. I asked a couple of therapists who are also from a Hispanic backgrounds, and they agreed that they rarely experience curiosity about their culture from mental-health therapists who work in their agencies. I believe we need to become aware of the ethnocentrism and biases that we may have in order to grow as mental-health family therapists who work in the reality of the USA, a country full of different cultures. Let's become aware and let's get real. My experience is probably similar to the experience of a lot of people who came from another culture. Don't we need to learn to be empathic and caring as therapists?

To be culturally sensitive is to be genuinely curious and understand that there are a lot of ways to do one thing—that there are many answers to one question—many paths that lead to the same solution. In China, they eat with chopsticks; in India, with their hands; in the Middle East, they eat on the floor; and in America, they eat in their cars. So you can be disgusted because it's different, or you can look at these differences and say, "Ugh, they're wrong, or they are stupid." This is cultural insensitivity to think that your way is better, right, and smarter. With this attitude, you are a person who doesn't like differences and feels threatened by them. All the cultural "knowledge" you have won't make a difference, because there is a lack of appreciation for differences. If you read twenty books about culture, but in the bottom of your heart, you don't accept that people from other cultures are not less or wrong, then you will not be culturally sensitive. On the other hand, you could be a person who has traveled little and read few books and be considered culturally sensitive by expressing a genuine interest and desire to understand another.

Being culturally sensitive is not being a person who thinks they know a culture because, in a book, they read the word "machismo" or "personalism," or that they are informed that Hispanics are too close with their families. Cultural sensitivity is to open your heart and mind and embrace differences…while celebrating them.

People from Hispanic cultures differ from country to country; however, one aspect they have in common is that they expect a therapist to be friendly, warm, and caring. They come with the assumption that you are the expert, but if you present yourself as detached, reserved, and stiff, this could be seen as threatening and unappealing. It's very important for the therapist to explain the importance of therapy, keeping appointments, making a commitment to weekly sessions. It's also important to emphasize working as a team, keeping your word as well as appointments, and having a strict cancellation policy. Families need to understand that when they give their word, they need to follow through. Missing appointments or canceling is a common issue among low-socioeconomic-status Hispanic populations and should be dealt with upfront and made very clear.

It should be made clear that any appointment with the therapist is just as important as an appointment with a doctor, an attorney, or an appointment with a welfare social worker. I explain that it's a commitment, and that it's extremely important. I make it understood that I am very busy and I value my time, as do they, and I don't like to fail. I don't like to work with people who don't like to work, so the cancellation policy is very strict. I take at least fifteen minutes emphasizing it during the first session, and then I keep reminding them each session, for five minutes, until they really get it and don't need to be reminded.

Role-modeling parenting skills are also key because parents from Hispanic cultures often use yelling, shaming, and hitting to discipline and teach their children. They need to learn parenting skills. The concept of boundaries is different from the American understanding of boundaries. For example, loyalty, shame, and a sense of obligation to the family of origin often create dysfunction and conflict because parents tend to be over-involved with their own biological family than with their own family or spouse. In the Hispanic culture, it is also very important what other people and family members think about you. This can create a lot of grief, because they let others define who they are, which can result in high anxiety or depression. So, decreasing the power that others have on their self-esteem should also be a focus of treatment.

In general, Hispanic people can be very expressive physically; hugging, kissing, touching, so it would be advised that a therapist develop a comfort level with that and be able to promote this kind of closeness.

Experiential and emotional work is very appropriate. Be aware that, as a therapist, you are going to be a team player in the family. The most important quality is to be genuine, real, and authentic in a way that is engaging, embracing, and expresses a commonality as human beings. What I want to say is, don't confuse culture with pathology. If all of us become committed to looking at the big picture and the process, and become genuinely culturally aware, our services for multicultural clients will be more productive and fruitful.(Cabouli.L,2005)

CHARACTERISTICS OF SOME CULTURES

Latino Family Characteristics

The Hispanic population is heterogeneous in nature. It is comprised of various groups of people with different backgrounds. These groups of people represent different historical, economic, political, and racial perspectives.

Regarding Mexicans, the physical proximity of Mexico to the United States allows these individuals to return easily to their homeland. In addition, the proximity of the two countries has also led to many Mexicans entering the United States illegally.

The reputation of the family as a whole is important to traditional Hispanic families. There is a double-standard applied, which dictates that men must work, and women must remain at home. There are tasks that are undertaken solely by women, such as child-rearing and housekeeping. The role of the man is to provide income for the household and to make the major family decisions. The cultural pattern of machismo is demonstrated by a man's virility, courage, and manliness. The women of the family are to be kept at home, and daughters are often prohibited from dating. In the past ten to fifteen years, there have been changes in these traditional patterns, mostly due to women entering the workforce in increasing numbers. Women now contribute more to the financial structure of the family and are making more decisions in the household. In the workplace, most Hispanics value economic independence and achievement (Altarriba and Bauer 1998).

Hispanics tend to prefer interpersonal relationships in groups that are nurturing, loving, intimate, and respectful. Their cultural value of allocentrism emphasizes these needs. Allocentrism is associated with high levels of conformity, mutual empathy, willingness to sacrifice for the welfare of the group, trust among members of the group, and high levels of interdependence. An important Hispanic value is one that promotes pleasant and non-conflicting social relationships. Religion is also an important part of life for traditional Hispanics in the United States, and is a way of maintaining the cultural identity (Altarriba and Bauer 1998).

Respect, or *respeto*, is an important value in these families. Elders are treated courteously and generally revered. Close relationships are also maintained with relatives and godparents, known as *compadres*. These people would replace the parents if something happened to them, and they could also help economically. Extended family is also very important. In many cases, it would be helpful to counsel the entire family and to note the family's sensitivity to external pressures (Altarriba and Bauer 1998). "Some studies have found that less acculturated Hispanic Americans perceive counselors with a greater degree of ethnic similarity as more favorable sources of help than Anglo Americans" (Altarriba and Bauer, 396). Altarriba and Bauer recommend a present-centered orientation for Hispanics that is active, spontaneous, and expressive in emotions and desires. The authors also pointed out that the color of the skin affects the way in which Hispanics are accepted into the American society; meaning it would be easier for a light-skinned Hispanic than for a dark-skinned one to gain acceptance. When Mexican Americans have similar characteristic to North American Indians and African Americans, they experience more prejudice and discrimination.

Characteristics of African American Families

The four main areas of difference between black African-American families and other ethnic groups include the African-American legacy, the history of slavery, racism and discrimination, and the victim system (Boyd-Franklin 1989). Kinship ties make up what is one of the most enduring and important aspects of African-American culture. The fact that people were captured and brought to this country as slaves was, among other things, disruptive, and it destroyed the kinship bonds and traditions. People could not marry, and their children were sold; they were sexually abused. Despite these conditions, they created their own rituals. "Slavery set the tone for black people to be treated as inferior; skin color was the badge of difference" (Boyd-Franklin, 10).

Poverty is an issue, but middle-class African-American people continue experiencing discrimination. Pinderhughes (1982) explains how the victim system works:

> A victim system is a circular feedback process that exhibits properties, such as stability predictability, that are common in all systems. This particular system

threatens self-esteem and reinforces problematic responses to community, families, and individuals. The feedback works as follows: Barriers to opportunity and education limit the chance of achievement and employment; this, in turn, leads to poverty and stresses that affect relationships in the family members' roles. This limited individual growth and limited opportunity for families to satisfy their own needs or to organize and improve the community's limited resources are bringing, as a result, the improbability of supporting families properly. The community itself becomes an active disorganizing influence, a breeder of crime and pathologies, and a cause of additional debility. (Pinderhughes, 109)

There are some controversies regarding race and class affecting Black people. Wilson (1987) argued that race has become less important than class. Even though some authors have described the African-American family as chaotic and unstable, authors such as White (1972) have researched black culture more positively. White described black families as "matriarchal," with strong kinship bonds, a strong work orientation, flexible roles, high achievement orientation, and strong religious affiliation. The kinship network is effective in providing children the emotional and economic support that they require.

Resistance to therapy is common for many black families—or the idea of being under treatment. A large number of black families label the experience of going to therapy as "crazy." A significant number of those families are not referred, but rather, are sent to therapy by courts, schools, or welfare officers. Additionally, there is the concept of privacy and of keeping family matters within the family. The suspicion and resistance exhibited by black families was described by Grier and Cobbs (1968, as cited in Boyd-Franklin 1989) as "a healthy cultural paranoia" (Cobbs, 19). This term encompasses their mistrust of people who are different by color, socioeconomic status, and lifestyle; therefore, building trust is the main concern in a therapeutic treatment before interventions can commence. Empowerment and therapeutic change are the most important treatment goals. This means helping people gain the ability to make their own decisions concerning their lives, as well as the lives of their children, thus achieving significant changes for themselves. It is important to understand that, when a therapist works with a family, he or she is working with the whole extended family (Boyd-Franklin 1989).

Asian American Family Characteristics

It must be taken into account that Asian-American people come from different groups and differ in terms of immigration history, educational level, economic and religious backgrounds, and degree of acculturation. Traditional Western psychotherapeutic approaches based on the assumption of individuation, independence, self-disclosure, verbal expression of feelings and long-term insight therapy may counter Asian-American values of self-independence, self-control, repression of emotions and short-term, result-oriented solutions (McGoldrick et al. 1996).

Kim (1985) recommended an integrated family therapy orientation from Haley's strategic and Minuchin's structural therapies. Ho (1987) recommended Bowen's intergenerational perspective and Satir's cognitive approach to "teach" family members to recognize the family's rules.

In Asian cultures, the family, rather than the individual, is the major unit of society. The family is the support validation and stabilization. It is important to understand that the Confucian ideology of harmony and interdependence is an integral part of Asian culture; the eldest son and the father have dominant roles. Marriages traditionally were arranged, and it was acceptable for men who had power in society to have concubines. The parent-child relationship was more important than the marital dyad. Shame and respect were used to control children. Women were self-sacrificing and over-involved with the children. (McGoldrick et al. 1996).

Contemporary Chinese-American families are one-child families that have replaced the extended family system. The family is less patriarchal; the mother shares the decision-making with the father. Romantic relationships have replaced arranged marriages, and children leave their homes (McGoldrick et al. 1996).

Japanese families are highly characterized by hierarchies and respect for age and seniority; cohesion and harmony are valued more than individual achievement. Korean families are also highly hierarchical. Parents guide, while children obey and respect. Marriage is considered the joining of two families rather than individuals. Parental consent is mandatory. The mother-in-law/wife relationship is generally complicated, because the mother is protected by her son and is critical of her daughter-in-law. In contrast, the relationship of son-in-law with parents-in-law is usually not a cause for conflict, due to low expectations. The way problems are confronted is either "right" or "wrong," and for this reason solution skills are limited. Frustration is managed frequently through the use of alcohol, which can extend the conflict to violence. Male children are very important in Korean families. Koreans are hot tempered and easily offended, gregarious, and humorous (McGoldrick et al. 1996).

Vietnamese families are very involved with their kinship, because the majority went through great suffering; losing everything they had before coming to America. It is important to bear in mind that this population reserves outside intervention as a last resource. In America, Vietnamese men lose power due to the financial independence of the women, and children are encouraged to be financially independent as soon as they can. They become intermediaries and interpreters for their parents. The result is additional confusion in the family system (McGoldrick et al. 1996).

Cambodian families have had a difficult history of war, trauma, and loss; consequently, a large portion of that population came to America with posttraumatic stress disorder. For Cambodians, conflict needs to be avoided at all cost, therefore they will not be straightforward in their attitude. This results in their being passive, or in their avoiding certain behavioral attitudes when dealing with anger. Nonetheless, they are willing to overlook what they consider aggressive or incorrect behavior if they perceive that the individual means well. They are very concerned with harmony and politeness. The social structure is based on the extended family, and on a highly stratified social relationship. The husband is the leader of the family, and the eldest son has a privileged position. Siblings refer to each other as "older" and "younger" brother/sister (McGoldrick et al. 1996).

SOME RESEARCH

Research Effectiveness of Systemic Approaches

Hazelrigg, Coope, and Bourduin (1987) reviewed the efficacy of various approaches for treating families. Their criterion was that the families include a minimum of one parent and one child. A control group was included, and a statistical analysis was performed. The study's results show that family therapy was more effective than no treatment at all, or than an alternative treatment, such as individual or group therapy. Analysis of follow-up data, ranging from six weeks to three years, revealed that family therapy continues to be more effective as time goes by, but less so than immediately after treatment. The authors recommended that, in the future, researchers should try to determine which approaches are best suited to certain populations presenting specific problems.

In a survey study, Rait (1988) found that, in practice, 34 percent of the responding therapists used an eclectic approach, while 18 percent used a structural approach. 12 percent used a strategic approach, and 7 percent used a Bowenian framework. It is important to point out that family therapy will continue to survive and grow only if marriage and family therapists are willing to throw their stones into the pool of knowledge and understanding.

Research on Structural Therapy, Intergeneration and Experiential Terapy

There is almost no research on intergenerational Bowen therapy. Evidence for the effectiveness of extended family systems therapy rests on personal experience and clinical reports. Bowen's research with schizophrenic families was clinical observation, and was not a controlled study (Nichols and Schwartz 1998).

Framo (1981) reported that there is no outcome data of his intergenerational approach and stated that this theory is not for all clinical situations. Framo (1981) reported that he had done no systematic research on his treatment method.

Experiential therapists have shown a lack of interest in verifying their theories or their results. There are no empirical studies on experiential therapy; what is offered is anecdotal reports of successful outcomes (Duhl and Duhl 1979; Napier and Whitaker 1978).

While Minuchin (creator of structural family therapy) was the director of the Philadelphia Child Guidance Clinic, he developed a highly pragmatic commitment to research. Studies of psychosomatic children, along with Stanton's studies of drug addicts, show very clearly how effective structural family therapy can be. In *Families of the Slums*, Minuchin, Montalvo, Guerney, Rosman, and Shumer (1967) described the structural characteristics of low-socioeconomic-status families and demonstrated the effectiveness of family therapy within that population. Prior to treatment, mothers in patient families were found to be either excessive or insufficient in exercising control; their children were more disruptive than those in controlled families. Minuchin et al. classified the families as "enmeshed," or "disengaged." After treatment, these mothers used less cohesive control, yet were clearer and firmer. In this study, seven out of eleven families improved after six months to one year. There was no control group, and none of the families rated as disengaged showed improvement.

The strongest empirical support for structural therapy comes from a series of studies with psychosomatic children and drug addicts. Minuchin (1981) reported on one study that clearly demonstrated how family conflicts may precipitate ketatosis crisis in psychosomatic–type, diabetic children. An interesting investigation compared three groups in terms of their response to a sequence of stress interviews. In the baseline, the parents discussed family problems with their children absent. These families displayed different symptoms: psychosomatic problems, behavioral disorders, and normal behavior. The results showed that normal spouses had the highest level of confrontation, while psychosomatic spouses exhibited conflict-avoidance maneuvers. While the children observed their parents arguing behind a two-way mirror, they experienced a dramatic increase in the fatty-acid level of their blood. When they joined their parents, normal individuals and those with behavioral disorders continued behaving the same way they had before the children were present. The psychosomatic parents detoured the conflict either by drawing the children into the discussion, or by switching the discussion from themselves to the children. When this happened, the fatty-acid level of the parents fell, while the levels in the children increased. It can be concluded that parents use psychosomatic children in an attempt to relieve stress in their relationship.

Minuchin et al. (1978) summarized the results of treating fifty-three cases of anorexia with structural family therapy. After the treatment was completed, which included hospitalization followed by family therapy on an outpatient basis, forty-three anorexic children greatly improved, two somewhat improved, three showed no changes, two were worse, and three dropped out. There was no control group, but the results were still impressive.

Structural family therapy was shown to be an effective form of treatment for drug addicts and their families, as well as for asthmatic individuals and those with complicated cases of diabetes. When Stanton and Todd (1979) compared family therapy with a family placebo condition, individual therapy symptom reduction was more than double that achieved with other conditions. These positive effects could still be seen in follow-ups at six to twelve months.

Szapocznik and associates have conducted several studies evaluating the effectiveness of structural family therapy (Szapocznik et al. 1983, 1986; Szapocznik et al. 1989). There are several studies that show that structural therapy was effective for behavioral and drug problems with Hispanic boys. In studies that compared structural family therapy with psychodynamic play therapy for children ages six through twelve, it was found that structural therapy was as effective as play therapy in the short run, and more effective in the long run at a one-year follow-up. The study also indicated that on measures of family functioning, the structural therapy group remained the same at the end of therapy and after one year, while the psychodynamic group was worse in that measure (Szapocznik et al. 1989).

STRATEGIES FOR RETAINING THE CLIENTS IN MULTI-PROBLEM FAMILIES

It is significant to note that one of the most important challenges in therapy with multi-problem families is retaining and engaging clients. There is research that reports that retaining and engaging clients is one of the main problems that family therapists face. These two points are critical challenges. For example, in order to engage Latino families, Bean, Perry, and Bedell Bean (2001) recommended understanding the cultural value of personalism, which is an approach to interpersonal relationships where closeness is expected, people are valued over things, and interpersonal characteristics are emphasized over individual achievement. These families are more likely to trust their therapist when they do some self-disclosure.

Previous research on rates of engagement showed that only 22 percent of families seeking treatment for a youth behavioral problem actually completed the assessment (Coatsworth et al. 2001). Kazdin (1996) reported that 40 percent to 60 percent of participants who begin an intervention will terminate it prematurely. Because of retention problems, engagement is an important criterion for assessing an intervention's effectiveness.

At times, treating multi-problem families can be difficult and often unsuccessful. Because of this situation, McNeil and Herschell (1998) proposed some strategies, such as increasing structure to teach organizations skills, developing a routine for sessions, keeping the appointment at the same time and day, creating attendance contracts, setting realistic treatment goals, helping the family to value therapy, making it a very positive experience, praising the clients for appropriate behaviors, and giving them pertinent information.

There is research that evaluates the effectiveness of brief strategic family therapy (BSFT) in engaging and retaining families and youth in treatment in a community agency which provides both individuals and families with services based on having family members gain greater insight and understanding of one another. The agency teaches parenting skills, improves communication, and supports interventions. The results indicated that BSFT was more successful when contrasted with the community comparison (CC) condition that represented common engagement and treatment practices. Also, those engaged were more likely to remain in treatment until completion (71 percent versus 42 percent). In other words, families assigned to BSFT were two to three times more likely to become engaged in therapy and see it to completion. Of interest is the fact that the population of this study was mostly Hispanic (Coatsworth et al. 2001).

It can be concluded that whatever the initial presenting problem may be, the initial obstacle to change is resistance. Because of this, Coatsworth et al. (2001) argued that the same systemic and structural principles that apply to the understanding of treatment should be applied to the understanding of a family's resistance to engagement. The solution to overcoming resistance lies in restructuring the family's patterns of interaction that permit the resistance to exist. Only then can therapists begin to work toward achieving goals. For example, a disengaged parent who is reluctant to attend therapy may also be maintaining the behavioral problem by undermining the directive of the spouse, via the adolescent. Joining begins with the therapist's first contact with the family and involves the task of engaging family members in treatment. Joining may entail using an agenda addressing the family's necessities (Coatsworth et al. 2001). To break maladaptive family interactions, therapists use techniques, such as reframing, reversals, detriangulation, and shifting boundaries and alliances. By doing this, therapists attempt to alter those family interactions that keep family members from working together effectively. Resistant families have intense marital conflicts, and the disengaged parent is concerned that in family therapy the focus will be on the conflict and not what he perceives to be the problem regarding the adolescent's behavior. By allying with the mother, the therapist can direct her to interact with her reluctant spouse in a more adaptable manner, which may help to assure the spouse that the focus will be on the child. For example, when working with Hispanic families, the clinician identifies the subset of family interaction patterns that occur in families that are difficult to deal with: (a) the powerful patient, (b) the disengaged parent, (c) the caller protecting the system, and (d) therapy as an exposé (Coatsworth et al.).

MARITAL SATISFACTION AND CHILD PSYCHOPATHOLOGY

Another study reviews the association between individual and marital conflict (Halford, Bouma, Kelly, and Young 2000). These findings are controversial for the systemic family point of view.

> Young (1999) reported that most of the studies that assess the relationship between marital distress and anxiety disorders have been conducted on women with phobias, agoraphobias, or panic disorders, and he refutes the systemic perspective that women's anxiety disorders maintain the stability of the relationship with a dysfunctional male. (Halford et al., 187)

Young (1999, as cited in Halford et al. 2000) reported that the reduction of anxiety symptoms in women suffering from these disorders increases marital satisfaction and functioning of the male partner.

There are some studies that compared perceived marital quality among couples in which one, both, or neither spouse met the criteria for one of the anxiety disorders. Researchers found relationships between anxiety disorder and marital satisfaction, but findings varied depending on whether women or men were experiencing the problem. When a man experiences a phobia, low marital satisfaction has been reported for both women and men; however, marital satisfaction was not low for women or men when it was the woman who experienced the phobia. Regarding panic attacks, marital satisfaction was low for both men and women (Halford et al. 2000).

> A distressed marriage is a strong predictor of the possibility of developing depression, particularly for women. Marital problems are strongly associated with the risk of dysphoria, adjustment disorder with depressed mood, and non-psychotic major depression. There is a slight association between psychotic depression and marital dissatisfaction. Couples who experience ongoing marital difficulty have high rates of psychological disorders, depression in wives, and alcohol abuse in husbands. (Halford et al. 2000, 181)

Additional research suggests that marriage is associated with better mental health in men and worse mental health in women. However, individuals suffering from severe psychological disorders are less likely to have a good marriage or even have a relationship. Some authors even suggest that marriage may be harmful to the mental health of women (Hafner 1985; Weissman and Klerman 1987).

There is interesting research about parental quality and well-being in relation to the parent-child relational quality in Chinese adolescent adjustment. In this study, researchers found that marital quality predicts parental well-being (Shrek 2000). Even though marital quality predicted parental well-being, marital quality and well-being for a father (but not for a mother) predicted parental-child relational quality. An interesting finding was that parental influence appears to have more influence in adolescent adjustment. A survey of literature shows that research consistently found marital conflict or well-being to be related to child adjustment. The findings of the study cited above are important because they show that gender differences in marital well-being for men were related to the quality of relationship between adolescent and parental well-being, while for women, this was not the same. Adolescent relational quality for a father was found to be a predictor of adolescent, psychological well-being. In other words, if a father has a good relationship with his wife, it is related to having a good relationship with the adolescent; therefore, the teenager will exhibit psychological well-being. In this study, the common belief is challenged that mothers are more important than fathers in influencing adolescent development. It is important to point out that this study was conducted only with Hong Kong Chinese couples, and the findings cannot be generalized to all populations (Shrek 2000).

BOTTOM LINE

After going through the process of understanding the model the stages, the different models that have been integrated, the different exercises and techniques, something about culture, I believe I have successfully explained my meaning.

I want this book to be as concrete as possible, as descriptive, and as direct as my model is. I hope I achieve my goal to be clear enough.

I am aware that many of my propositions go against much of what we learn in school. Our litigious country makes our work as therapists a difficult job; we learn to see that sometimes we really don't do anything, and we become enabled by our own fears.

I feel fear when the systems are being de-balanced because I know how my clients feel, and I know that the homeostatic process is powerful, and I am being paid to help and promote change in order to help this group of people overcome their tendency of staying in their comfort zone. On the other hand, my eighteen years of experience gives me the confidence that 80 percent of the time, we achieve this goal. I have also learned that not everybody wants to grow a lot; some people want different levels of growth than others, and I have learned to be respectful of that, too. To be truthful, this was the most difficult thing to learn and accept.

Strategic Experiential family therapy is the result of my eighteen years of work in two countries.I try this type of work with North Americans, and my interns apply this model in to this population with very good results.

The research done in this model so far was a qualitative phenomenologic-ethnographic approach conducted with ten families who were referred to a school-based program in southeast San Diego, due to the symptomatology of a child in the six-to-seventeen age range. The interviews were held within a one-year period after therapy had terminated and the families were treated with an integrative approach created by the researcher. Phenomenological research was the main point of the research endeavors (Polkinghorne 1989). For the purpose of this study, phenomenological research procedures were applied based on Colaizzi's (1978) systematic approach. The researcher followed a four-step procedure after transcribing the interviews. First, she read all interviews several times, until a sense of familiarity with the material had been attained. Second, she independently identified the sections in each interview that had commonality. Third, she searched for units of meaning within each interview and across all interviews. Fourth, she developed generalizations that unified several units of meaning into broader categories, and those were abstracted to a higher level of generalization.(Goberman- Cabouli. L,2003)

MY PHENOMENOLOGICAL RESEARCH STUDY

My dissertation(Goberman-Cabouli.L , 2003) was a phenomenological study, where people who underwent this treatment were interviewed after the end of therapy.

This is what people said about their experience with Strategic Experiential family therapy. The result of a phenomenological study done by nine families who underwent this type of treatment.(Goberman- Cabouli.L,2003)

COMPREHENSIVE ACCOUNT OF THEMES

The experience of the families who underwent SEFT(Goberman-Cabouli.L , 2003): must be premised upon the fact that there were three general category(a) the overall impression of the families undergoing the treatment (themes numbered 1-3 and 5-11) (b) what they achieved in therapy (theme number 4), and (c) the families' experience with what the therapist did (themes numbered 12-15). These three categories involved a total of fifteen themes, some of which had sub-themes.

An in-depth analysis of the semi-structured interview transcriptions revealed fifteen themes, some of which had sub-themes. Below is a list of the various themes, followed by illustrative excerpts from the interviews.(Goberman-Cabouli,L;2003)

Theme #1—Overall understanding of what therapy was about (i.e., feelings and ideas about the purpose of therapy.

Theme #2—Point of view before therapy, compared to after therapy (i.e., "I changed my point of view.").

Theme #3—Overall feelings about how change occurred in therapy.

    a. Little by little.
    b. Specific situation, time, or realization that change had occurred in other family members.
    c. Unknown how change occurred.

Theme #4—Effects of therapy as reported by family members.

    a. Awareness (e.g., "Therapy opened my eyes.").
    b. Better communication, problem-solving, and negotiating skills.
    c. Better management of compulsive behaviors and impulsivity.
    d. Improvement in relationships—safety in being "vulnerable" in front of each other, improved quality of marriage.
    e. Improved concepts of self-definition (e.g., "I learned that my opinion counts.").
    f. Better parenting skills.
    g. Improvement in school matters (e.g., grades).

Theme #5—Impressions/feelings about difficulties in therapy and what made participants continue.

Thoughts/predictions about what therapy was going to be.

    a. Waste of time, conflict producing, worthless.
    b. Helpful.

Theme #7—Expressed complaints and fears about therapy by teenagers/children.

Theme #8—Overall feelings and ideas regarding being all together in the therapy room.

    a. Positive feelings.
    b. Negative feelings (e.g., arguing, disagreeing).

Theme #9—Understanding of our feelings about the problem being reframed as a family rather than individual problem; understanding the link between marital dysfunction or parental well-being and behavior in children/adolescents.

Theme #10—What participants said about family-of-origin issues, participation in the treatment of them, and insight.

Theme #11—What participants would do about future problems after therapy ended.

    a. Try to resolve the problems by themselves.
    b. Ask for some kind of treatment or help.

Theme #12—Opinions, feelings, and concepts about how family members viewed the therapist.

a. Therapist helped them to see what they were doing wrong and right.
  b. Therapist displayed warmth, empathy, and trustworthiness; treated participants as equal; self-disclosure.
  c. Therapist was like an expert/teacher/medical doctor/mediator—helped participants to bring order to their homes.
  d. Therapist saw reality of situation and confronted participants; therapist was active/strong/determined in pushing; therapist inspired respect.

Theme #13—Setting boundaries.

Theme #14—Therapist's sensitivity to issues of culture and language.

Theme #15—Participants' feelings and perceptions regarding how well the therapist understood the family's problem(s).

THEME #1

This theme involved an overall understanding of what therapy was about, including feelings and ideas about the purpose of therapy. Dialogue excerpts from all nine families are presented below.

Family #1.

Mother: Help us understand, make sense about your children, when your children don't listen, to tell the children to go to school. To go with someone that can advise your children so someone could follow.

Daughter: Is a good choice, to bare your frustration and confusion and tell someone about them. To get advice, to learn how to communicate better, to set goals and achieve them.

Family #2.

Mother: They taught us how to be parents to our children, to teach the kids to be good kids, and encourage them to go to school.

Father: They explained to us, helped us learn how to take care of the children. Sometimes we played games. I don't know how to explain the game, but it was fun—we all laughed together.

Mother: And they told us to tell the children to help us out. Example: helping to cook and clean the house, and give chores to each other. The therapist helped in the relationship with my husband—she helped us a lot. She also helped us with referrals of food and stuff that we need.

Family #3.

Father: I agreed to go to therapy because it really help us. Our therapist came and taught us about relationships.

Client: We talked all together about our differences. We talked about how we were; before I was aggressive with my dad—my dad was aggressive with me.

Mother: The therapist helped me a lot and all the family. I would recommend to a person to do therapy, because sometimes you think that things go right, and they don't go so right, and it is a good thing that someone from the outside sees the things, because from the inside you don't see them, and the person from the outside and you get surprised at how they can see the problem.

Younger Sister: It was a good opportunity to resolve our problems.

Family #4.

Mother: We went to the interviews, and the therapist set limits and said that each member must occupy a specific place in the home. She also explained how to get along with my husband; to talk often with him... The interviews were very helpful to us, because we didn't know many things, such as how to conduct ourselves with the children, how and when to obey them, how to listen to them, how to care for them. The fact is that—that personally—it was all work, work—with little time devoted to my children. But now, I pay them more attention. What they tell me, put—be in back of them—what's happening, what's not happening, and so forth. This is what family therapy is for.

Mother: There would be talks about what had happened to my daughter—nothing else. We needed help more than anything else. This is why we agreed to go. You must attend all the sessions. We would go because she would teach us to be better parents by giving us "tips" that we could put into practice. And above all, learn.

Mother: Well, he did this the first time. Then she started coming here to attend all of us. She gathered all of us together. She treated "R," and she treated both of us as a couple. That was her role.

Family #5.

Uncle: Yes, it's a program to determine how a family can better communicate or get a clearer understanding between the family members to bring them closer together.

Aunt: That means I would know how to deal with the family issues that were oppressing me at the time.

Family #6.

Stepfather: That it is good. It helps to improve. It helps you in your marital relationship. You learn how to relate with your family. You learn how to instruct yourself, because sometimes, you are ignorant regarding family matters, and you learn about it with your family, wife, and children. And with your own self. First, you would be going to the school in a certain time. One time, the therapist appeared, came to the house

Mother: I would tell them that is something very important for the marriage and for the children. You learn how to treat your children and your husband, also. At the beginning, I went with the purpose of my problems with your children, older son—to learn how to communicate with him and talk about drugs, sex, etc., what is wrong or right. So I got into counseling, and it came out my marital problems—that you go for something and then more things began to appear. After that, my husband came to therapy, and he became part of it.

Client: I would recommend people to go to counseling. If you go to school and your grades are low, or you have problems with your parents, you resolve your problems. At the beginning, my mother began to ask questions about a program, and then we met our therapist.

Family #7.

Client: She used to ask us questions [about] how school was, if we did something wrong, if we were punished or beaten.

Younger Sister: She asked us if my mother hit us.

Family #8.

Father: Counseling teach me skills teach me about the system of my family, how it is, I would tell a friend that if they go the family system would work better.

Mother: It teaches the family system. They told you that the marital dyad is important, it help the family to grow.

Family #9.

Mother: Well, I would say to that family that, if they are in crisis, going to the program would be very helpful. The therapist has good techniques for the person that has depression, personal problems, problems with themselves, and with the teenagers.

Father: The therapist is a nice, polite lady, and she tries to help you [by] asking a lot of questions that make you feel healthier in every type of problem.

Older Brother: I went with the therapist because I need her to help with my anger, and I do not hit things like I did before. And if one friend asks me, I would tell him to go, because it relieves the problems.

Client: I would say that the program was very good to take things out and how my brother said it is good to go to the program—it helps you a lot—it helps families. Sometimes we went to the school for therapy; others, the therapist came to our home. We told things to each other, if things were okay or not in the home. She let us spell all things out.

THEME #2

This theme involved the families' point of view before therapy, as compared to after therapy. Dialogue excerpts from families #1, #2, #3, #4 #6, #7, #8, and #9 are presented below.

Family #1.

Daughter: It changed my point of view, because we understand each other a little more. My mother is nagging less, and I put myself down less.

Family #2.

Father: Yes, it was different. For example, before, I allowed my son to do things on his own, without questioning a lot. I don't allow them to do everything, because we need to have some control. Now I asked them more where they are going, when they will be back—like dropping "S" at the library and he's supposed to return at 5:00 p.m., but didn't. Then I go and look for him.

Family #3.

Mother: I think that before, we saw the problems a little bit exaggerated. We used to fight a lot, but not anymore. We talk about things. We did not resolve problems in the past. I was very angry, and I answered in a bad way my husband and my daughter. I did not know the problems that were going on.

Family #4.

Mother: It really changed my point of view of my problems. But the hate for the guy that abused my child, it did not go away. No therapist, even with all the degrees that the therapist has, could take from me this feeling. But right now it is all about supporting my daughter, and that is like a book that I already closed. In reference to other problems, the therapy helped us to change, to give a better solution to our problems.

Client: It was very good, I enjoyed it. It helped me very much. It changed my way of being.

Family #6.

Mother: When I left the session, I used to see things differently—things that were extremely important to me that were, in reality, small, and I remember I began to think, "Because of this, I am angry. Because of this, I have a problem. I would let this go."

Family #7.

Mother: Yes, I saw the problems in a different way, like if I have more peace, like if I am more calm—not only violence in the house. The problems are not like before; they got resolved, I am calmer in my home.

Family #8.

Father: We have a different perspective, for example, before therapy, I got angry and yelled at my kids, and after therapy, I think before react.

Father: Yes, I did change my point of view.

Father: Before therapy, I saw my daughter as impossible. During the course of therapy, I saw that she was scared of going to a group home.

Mother: It is hard to me to say, I but thought, before therapy, that my daughter is bad. She was a bad girl that did bad things. After therapy, I noticed that I don't see her as bad; more neutral.

Family #9.

Older Brother: To me, [it] was a change in my perspective of life, because I was feeling very bad. All my friends from Latino America were killed. I was the only one that stayed alive. The advice the therapist gave me made me think a lot [that] I did not want to die. I take advantage of her advice, and I change.

Older Brother: I said she made me change my path. She changed the family. We were all depressed. We are not depressed anymore.

Mother: Personally, I felt very depressed. All what happened or not happened was indifferent to me. The therapist made me see things differently—took my medicine, because I take antidepressant. It doesn't bother [me] any more that they [the children] try to put pressure over me.

Client: I thought my problems were different. They were not as big as I thought.

THEME #3

This theme involved overall feelings about how change occurred in therapy. ***Theme #3A*** was little by little; dialogue excerpts from families #3, #7, and #8 are presented below.

Family #3.

Father: I felt it was little by little. The therapist was helping us, explaining things, errors about oneself, the way you should treat your children —nice things she used to tell us. And little by little, and even without noticing, I was behaving better with my daughter and with my wife—without noticing, I began to change.

Family #7.

Mother: It was little by little. It was no special day—well, the same day that she told me that she was happy about my changes and that I react. That was the time I separated from my live-in boyfriend. I used to date these guys that do nothing. They were like a burden to me. And I realize that they were good for nothing, and create more problems for me that solutions.

Family #8.

Father: I think I changed gradually.

Theme #3B involved a specific situation, time, or realization that change had occurred in other family members. Dialogue excerpts from all families except #7 follow:

Family 1.

Daughter: [talking about change in therapy] One time, she [the therapist] explained to me how my mother feels. The therapist told me that my mother acted like this because of my mother's child history. She was hurt a lot of times and mistreated, and she wants the best for us for our future, because she did not have a good one, so she wanted a good future for us.

Mother: I remember I slow down in my complaints.

Family #2.

Father: I understand more after about midway through the treatment. Listening to them—they explain [about] the children. I have less worries now, but still worry and still pay a lot of attention and watch them closely.

Family #3.

Client: I never thought to leave therapy, because I felt the change. I felt things were changing. I saw my parents changing, and things got better.

Client: I think it was not—things did not happen in one second. It's not that we went there and we changed in one second. It was hard work for us, and time. We all put effort into it. When the therapist ended treatment, the real change occurred. I feel we can live together better, and we don't have her to say, "Oh, 'A' misbehaved," etc. And everything fell into place, and we continue together.

Mother: At three or four months of beginning treatment.

Client: Yes, three or four months.

Family #4.

Mother: It was an important confrontation that we had. Neither my husband nor the therapist gave up. I wanted to cry, because my husband was saying that everything he was saying was the reality and how things need to be. When the therapist left the session, we said that you find the size of your shoes. Things really changed since that point.

Family #5.

Aunt: I remember when he started doing better in school, it started looking up. When he was turning around, I thought, "Hmmm, he's going to make it."

Aunt: I noticed he wasn't hanging with the same friends.

Aunt: He even started doing better in church, didn't he, baby? Started talking in church and stuff.

Aunt: You don't recall him talking in church? He would get up and do the Sunday school over you and stuff.

Uncle: I don't know. Did you do that?

Client: Yeah, I would.

Aunt: He would start doing it, though.

Uncle: After we took his clothes, he started doing better, keeping some of his commitments, like doing his chores more.

Aunt: Well, I noticed the last time she took his clothes, it was the first time I seen him cry, so I know there was a change, because he was Mr. Tough Man, but that day, he cried.

Family #6.

Stepfather: I remember that I realized that I was changing because of the children. "S" and my daughter, they were happier. It looks like they were smarter. Between us, I do not remember in what moment things began to change. I begin to see that "S" was improving at school, and as a human being, my daughter was also changing. She was smarter, happier, and more alive.

Mother: At the fourth session, or one month, "D" began to change a lot. He was different with me; he understood me more; he did more things. He talked with "S"; he tried to help him more, in his homework, explaining to him. Even though he came late and tired from work, he did that—then somehow stopped being possessive with me. Because he changed, I begin to say to myself, if he is changing, I would do it also. Sometimes we went back to being the ones that we were, and then we went back and arranged the problem again, but [it] was lighter, because we talk about things, what bothered us. And before, I used to stay silent and say nothing. At this time I don't do that anymore. He knows why I am pissed.

Client: As I said before, my grades began to change, and I stopped coming late to school, because if I continued to be like this, I would be in the records of the school, and I began to think.

Family #8.

Mother: I saw that my children respect the rules more and thought more before acting; they are not so oppositional anymore. I notice that my husband changed; he is not so upset as before.

Family #9.

Mother: The pivotal moment was when my older son decided to go back to school. I threatened him [about] what I was going to do if he did not go to school, and he decided to go. He decided to change. I couldn't believe it. I thought I was going to die of happiness that my children changed. I did not know when and how but my children changed. For two years, I was saying to him to go to school, and abruptly someone made a click in his head, or he got tired of me telling that over and over.

Older Brother: When I began to go to school, everything began to change. I began to meet a lot of people, because before I didn't know anybody, and my depression disappeared. I am not depressed anymore, and I have a lot of friends.

Client: When I began to see that we began to change—that there was a difference between us. There was a difference between us; we began to communicate—began to see my mother addressing me, and I began to feel better. When my mother stopped being upset, all began to change.

Theme #3C was that it was unknown how change occurred. Following is a dialogue excerpt from family #3:

Younger Daughter: I don't know how she helped us. Everything occurred so fast, and I did not realize how I did not want my parents to know what I was going through. But she took all my information out—I don't know how.

Mother: I felt very happy with the therapist. I don't know how things began. I don't know how things began to change. It was without me noticing. My husband was involved in the treatment.

THEME #4

This theme involved the effects of therapy as reported by family members. ***Theme #4A*** dealt with awareness (e.g., "Therapy opened my eyes"). Dialogue excerpts from families #1, #2, #3, #4, #5, #6, and #9 follow:

Family #1.

Mother: I understand that I am too concerned about my daughter. I should relax, but it was very difficult not to be concerned about my daughter.

Family #2.

Father: When the therapist came to our family, she brightened the family, by the help—the things she said and the questions she asked.

Father: Before, it felt like a frog in a big pond, the head barely sticking above the water, feeling confused and lost—about to drown. But now, we have a clear picture.

Mother: I see [therapy] as opening our eyes and helpful to the family.

Family #3.

Mother: A person like the therapist helped us. If not, we would not be able to stop being in the dark.

Younger Sister: All we're saying is what we feel. We said what was going on, what we felt, because we didn't have communication.

Younger Sister: She helped us know how all of us felt. Like when my sister talked, she told us a lot of things that I did not know about. Like my father—my father really surprised me. I did not know a lot of things about my father. They hide a lot of things from me. In that setting I realized how everyone felt and discovered a lot of stuff.

Client: I began to ask my father how he felt. I never knew how my mother or father felt, why they acted with me in the way they did—I did not understand any reasons.

Family #4.

Client: I believe she did, because at the beginning everything was dark, very dark. There is a point that you get cold. Today I think twice [about] what I am going to say, I don't answer whatever… I think what I would say, and if it makes sense, I say it.

Family #5.

Aunt: For me, it made me check myself out, and it also made me realize some of the points I wasn't aware of, and it also helped me to have a better relationship with my husband.

Aunt: Yes. I used to talk real, real loud. I don't talk loud as I used to anymore, so that stood out, and she showed me, and she was saying, like my husband always told me, too, "You're going to have a heart attack getting excited and stuff." And I think I saw that, and that stood out more than all that stuff.

Family# 6.

Stepfather: You begin to learn, to learn how things need to be. Is very difficult to give up your pride time. But you realize that it is good. We as people are difficult—that for keeping on in a relationship, you should set the pride aside.

Family #9.

Client: All of us began to see the reality the therapist opened to all of us our eyes. We all were going in a bad direction. This is what happened.

Mother: I was paying too much attention. I learned how to give them the right amount of attention. Before, they wanted to be the one in charge; they thought they were my boss, and right now everything is under control.

Theme #4B dealt with better communication, problem-solving, and negotiating skills. Following are dialogue excerpts from families #1, #3, #4, #5, #6, #8, and #9:

Family #1.

Mother: It helps both of us to communicate. The therapist give us advice, we said yes, yes, yes, and then we did not follow through learn not to talk so much not to hit my kids.

Family #3.

Client: She made me think a lot. She told me a lot of things—"Why are you acting like this?" or "Why are you doing that?" She told me how to communicate with my dad. She made me laugh and cry.

Father: To tell the truth, the fact that we communicated with each other, that we were honest with each other—we were in a bad situation.

Client: That we all talked—the therapist went straight to the point.

Father: It was a good technique to resolve problems. She knew she needed to put all of us together. She did good. She put all of us eye to eye, and she made us talk. Then she looked at us and described what we were doing.

Younger Sister: Yes, she taught us how to resolve problems.

Family #4.

Client: The therapy taught me more to communicate with my father, and the advice of the therapist helped me. Because if my father gets angry and said something that you know is not as he is saying, I leave him until he calms down, and after that, I say to him that I thought the advice of the therapist was helpful.

Mother: To speak with them—we spoke very little. To chat with my husband, with whom I had little communication.

Mother: I learn to listen to my children, to believe in them because they were telling me the truth.

Family #5.

Uncle: The fact of getting together and communicating the matter that we need to better understand each other and listen to each other.

Uncle: I thought it was to bring about better communication among our family to help us really understand each other. We might have been saying the same things, but we needed a mediator.

Uncle: Right, I was able to listen to what other people had to say more. That's one of the key elements in really getting better communication, as you know. You have to be willing to listen. Most people don't listen. They want to spot me out whenever they feel an opening. They're not willing to sit back and be relaxed and take their turn and say whatever they need to say.

Family #6.

Client: I began to change. At the beginning, I had no communication with my stepfather. He did not talk to me, so I did not talk to him. After therapy, we began to talk more. I began to notice that he was talking more. I don't know, but little by little, he began to talk to me and told me that he was treating me the same way

> that his stepfather used to treat him. Because I was doing bad in school, I began to ask him questions, and we began to talk.

Mother: "D's" [husband] participation in the counseling was very important. Sometimes we went back to be the ones that we were, and then we went back and arranged the problem again, but [it] was lighter, because we talk about things, what bothered us. And before I used to stay silent and say nothing. At this time I don't do that anymore. He knows why I am pissed.

Mother: When I think that I remember things, we talk in counseling, and I said I would continue because of this or that, and I would try to talk and talk and find a middle point for the sake of my marriage. I don't know.

Mother: She did a lot. She taught me a lot. She explained a lot of things. She wanted us to learn how to talk, how to negotiate to find a middle point, because we were not on the same page. He did something —I did something else. She taught us to give up sometimes and to talk, talk, talk. She really helped me.

Family #8.

Father: I felt happy that there was somebody to help us solve our problem. I felt like I was crazy, because I didn't know how to solve my problem. I felt like I was stupid, too.

Father: The therapist taught me some skills to communicate with my children. For example, the same meaning of the question with a different way to express it has different results.

The skill helps me to speak in a positive way. The communication skills were helpful.

Mother: The most helpful were the communication skills. It was improving our relationship with our children.

Family #9.

Mother: I knew how to resolve the problems better. The therapist taught me things that I did not know existed; how to manage my problems, or not to care so much what people said about me, because I was the type of person that, if someone said something about me, I took it very personally. She taught me how to take problems in a different way with my children and husband.

Theme #4C dealt with better management of compulsive behaviors and impulsivity (e.g, alcohol problems, anger). Dialogue excerpts from families #1, #3, #5, #7, #8, and # 9 follow:

Family #1.

Mother: I learned not to hit them [her children].

Family #3.

Mother: When "A" gets mad, I say, "Leave her alone. It's going to be over."

Father: When she gets stubborn, I ignore her. I don't get mad. I take it like a joke. I need to be calm, and everything will get back to normal.

Father: I am very sorry and ashamed, because I used to yell at her, and I hit her. I am very sorry.

Family #5.

Aunt: Yes. I used to talk real, real loud. I don't talk loud as I used to any more, so that stood out, and she showed me, and she was saying, like my husband always told me, too, "You're going to have a heart attack getting excited and stuff." And I think I saw that, and that stood out more than all that stuff.

Family #7.

Mother: She really helped me in that matter—I was very violent, and that helped me a lot. I feel a lot calmer right now. I don't drink anymore, and I think more carefully.

Mother: Our relationship changed. Our way of relating to each other changed. I am a nervous person. I got anger easily and had no control. Through her telling me, "Don't react like that—take it easy—if you get so angry, it will affect your health," and that it hurts my daughters. She gave us examples of how to live in harmony with my daughters, how to treat them; and then I began to analyze, and yes, I love them a lot. She used to say, "Give them your love, build their trust, so that everything they see in the streets or what happens to them, they can tell you. Give them trust so they can trust in you." And I am grateful to the therapist—

Family #8.

Mother: I learned to deal with the kids. We learn that if we have a problem, we should not discuss in front of my kids. We should not pull the kids in the middle of our arguments.

Family #9.

Older Brother: I did not improve in the other therapy that I underwent. Instead of helping, they made me more ingrate—did not help me—and I thought that it was going to be the same. But it was the opposite, what the therapist said—was the opposite of what the other said. And I did it because of her: I go to work, I go to the school, and on the weekends I go to "R" ... with my friends.

Older Brother: For example, I slept in the car yesterday and I was in a bad mood, and I told my mother, "What do you have to eat?" And she answered, "No, there is nothing yet," and I got mad. Ten minutes later, I was okay and my anger was gone, and I was smiling. Another example: Today I got an appointment in immigration, and the appointment was early in the morning, and that bothers me, and I feel angry. But lately I don't think about it anymore; I put everything in the past, and I stopped being angry.

Mother: My daughter was behaving like a teenager. She was rebelling: "I am leaving the home with my friend." She doesn't know what was she talking about, and I was like, "I am going to hit you." That was my only thought. But after, she changed. I don't know what happened, but she changed, like with magic. Sometimes the therapist talk with [the client] without me. I don't know what she did.

Father: I used to drink, but little by little, I stopped, because I work, and I am not a drunk person anymore.

Mother: He doesn't have time anymore for that, because he works.

Father: The therapy was good for us. I used to drink a lot; the therapist helped me a lot. She used to say, "Don't drink; if not, I will need to put you in rehab." I did not work; I used to work in the kitchen, and right know I work again—thought it was a good idea to put myself together. Was scared of the therapist, because I thought she was going to nag because I was drinking, but I stopped drinking. Before I did not work, I spend the day thinking; I am currently working, and I don't drink.

Theme #4D dealt with improvement in relationships, safety in being "vulnerable" in front to each other, an improved quality of marriage, and understand each other better. Dialogue excerpts from families #1, #2, #3, #4, #5, #6, 8, and # 9 follow:

Family #1.

Daughter: It helps me to understand my mother better. I hear how my mother felt, how she was hurt, and see what make her happy, so I will try my best to make her happy, doing some of the things she wants me to do.

Family #2.

Father: She helped us [the relationship with wife] to brighten and love each other more.

Father: It was helpful in that we understand one another better.

Family #3.

Mother: She would never stay with us—she would have left the house. But finally, she finished high school, and she stayed with us. I am very happy about it, because she is doing very good in college, and she is with us.

Father: If not for the therapist, we would not be together. We had a lot of pressure.

Father: So we are all on the same page, to help the family get attached to each other.

Client: Therapy helped me to relate with my boyfriend.

Mother: She made us hug each other a lot.

Father: [The therapist said:] "Hug her and give her a kiss."

Father: The moment the therapist came into our lives, it was like a bomb was going to explode, and she helped us to find our way out.

Client: Before therapy, when my father got home, I was in the living room and went to my room. I never gave him a hug.

Family #4.

Client: It helped to talk things out without feeling ashamed.

Family #5.

Aunt: And it also helped me to have a better relationship—[relationships] tend to break, because these days these young people; it's hard [for them] to understand you.

Aunt: Finding out different points about myself. What I needed to do to improve my relationship—even myself.

Family #6.

Mother: First, I was doing very good. I began to learn things. Every time I went to the session, I liked it, because I was learning a lot of things. In that way, I was improving my marriage. A lot of time, I thought I did not want to be in the relationship. When I attended the session, I began to feel again that I wanted to fight for the relationship and stay in it. Time passed by, and I stopped thinking about leaving the relationship—I wanted to keep on. We went to therapy; we expressed what we feel; the therapist talked to us, and we left the place happier. The next day, we had a little problem, and the problem began to build. I did not do anything that the therapist taught us, because it was difficult, and I began to think again, "I don't want to be in this relationship."

Family #8.

Father: We learned that we should talk more; we fight less; we have more love.

Family #9.

Client: When I began the program, they realized that I wasn't the only problem in the home. I thought they saw [us] all together, so we can take out all that we have inside, in front of everybody. So we don't have secrets—no big ones, no small ones. I think they sent us all together to see if, all together, we can understand each other more, because we all know each other a lot.

Theme #4E dealt with improved concepts of self-definition, self-differentiation, and improved self-esteem (e.g., "I learned that my opinion counts"). Dialogue excerpts from families #3, #4, and #6 follow:

Family #3.

Mother: She took me back to my childhood and helped me process my traumas. She helped me in confronting problems that I was not willing to confront. She helped me a lot. I felt a lot of support from her. She helped me to mature.

Family #4.

Mother: Whatever he said had to be done. Not anymore, because now I ask him: "Why, because you say so?" I, too, have to give my point of view. Now, my opinion counts. Now everyone speaks up. "What do you think of this?" "What about that?" Not before—before, when Dad gave an order, it was carried out. This is helping me very much. I would like to continue with the therapy, because one learns something every day. Small incidents appear unexpectedly, and you have to cope with them. She helps you in resolving them.

Mother: I learned that, as a woman, you need to appreciate yourself. You don't need to give up on what you really think. I was the type of woman that, if my husband said green, I said green, even if he was wrong. Right now is different. And it was at that time, the therapist used to ask me what I was feeling, what was going on with me—that I don't need to be silent, that I need to have an opinion, that my voice also counts. We met and we couldn't find the place.

Client: She taught us that it was not only my father's opinion that counts. I learned that, if you want to succeed, you need to think of yourself.

Family #6.

Mother: I learned in the therapy how to appreciate myself and to stand up, and that created a problem. But the next session come, and we went back closer.

Stepfather: The most important thing I learned was to give up my pride, and I learned that was not so important that made things continue—I gave up on that. In therapy they gave you tips—is like a process of learning—and I learned that [it] was stupid to be so proud and stubborn. And it's true how I used to tell my therapist the pride is something that you feel, inside your body—is not in the outside, is in the inside. I cannot fake it. That is why it was difficult. I don't know how big pride is in other people, but mine is big.

Theme #4F dealt with better parenting skills. Dialogue excerpts from families #1, #2, #4, #5, #7, and #8 follow:

Family #1.

Mother: She helps me to understand the responsibility as a mother with a teenager. She helps me to teach the kids how to listen to me. I learned I need to support take care of my kids, feed them—want my kids to stay at home at a certain time.

Family #2.

Father: We learned our roles as parents. It's been better for our family.

Family #4.

Mother: With the younger of my children, I learned to do "time out." For my older daughter; to explain why does not need to do a certain thing, why I don't want her to go to a certain place. I learned that [by] talking with the therapist. I try to apply all that I learned.

Family #5.

Aunt: He has to remember that "D" used to play both of us, and I know that. He would play me against him and him against me.

Family #7.

Mother: The treatment I displayed with my daughters—I did not know how to treat them. I used to hit my children, and I stopped. I understood that did not win anything doing that, and that really helped me, I don't do it anymore. I know that it hurts them when I set consequences for their behavior, but that helps me a lot.

Family #8.

Father: It was not bad. The therapist taught me how to solve my children's problems. I see things more clear right know, not to argue in-front of my children and learn to be more patient with my kids and have conversations with them.

Theme #4G concerned improvement in school matters (e.g., grades). Dialogue excerpts from families #3, #5, #6, and #9 follow:

Family #3.

Client: To improve in school with problems with my friends and with college.

Family #5.

Client: The good things—I guess she's saying it helped me get through school and helped me focus, but I didn't really like it.

Client: The only thing that probably really helped me and kept me focused [was] I knew I had to get my clothes back. I wanted my clothes, so I had to focus at school. That's about the only thing that really helped me was taking away my clothes.

Aunt: Also, I want to say, too, that if she hadn't come, I don't know if he would have really graduated, because it made us see a lot of what he needed to do to go in the right direction, because he was going in the wrong direction with his peers.

Family #6.

Client: I think that, yes, before I did not care about school, and I changed my grades when I was going to counseling, and I feel like improving and improving.

Client: She helped me with the school, how to have better grades, and she began to talk to "D." I don't know.

Family #9.

Mother: The pivotal moment was when my older son decided to go back to school. I threatened him [about] what I was going to do if he did not go to school, and he decided to go. He decided to change. I couldn't believe it. I thought I was going to die of happiness because my children changed. I did not know when and how, but my children changed. For two years, I was saying to him to go to school, and abruptly someone made a click in his head, or he got tired of me telling that over and over.

THEME #5

This theme was related to impressions/feelings about difficulties in therapy and what made participants continue. Dialogue excerpts from all families follow:

Family #1.

Mother: When my daughter was rebelling or disobeying me, the therapist helps me to understand why that was happening. Transportation and language barrier was difficult also.

Daughter: When we don't know how to help ourselves and us wants to avoid the problem. But we knew we needed help. It was difficult because both of us were stubborn. We need to give up a little bit to be better, for the whole family.

Mother: It was very difficult to see that my daughter would listen to someone and not to me.

Daughter: When we don't know how to help ourselves, and we want to avoid the problem. But we knew we needed help.

Family #2.

Father: No nothing was difficult. When we have appointment with the therapy, go to see their office in downtown and sometimes they come here to our house. Just sometimes my car broke down and [we] could not make it to the appointment. That was difficult.

Family #3.

Mother: When she confronted all of us together was the harder part, because we did not know what was going on. And we continued therapy, because she did these confrontations so well, we realized that we needed therapy—that we needed to overcome our difficulties that our family needed to be together as a unit. We are a family.

Client: At the beginning was the harder part—to begin, to make the decision of going to someone to help our family. Besides that, I went for one year, and it did not help me at all. When I began to observe the changes, I did not think about leaving therapy. It was difficult to begin, but not to continue. The first time she arranged to go to my home, I observed my mother, and all of them wanted to change the day—another day and another day. The therapist said, "Not another day—the day we arranged already is [when it] is going to be."

Family #4.

Mother: The harder part was to say what happened and find out more about it. We want to appreciate each other more, my husband and myself—we made the decision that therapy was good for the sake of the family—more for our daughter, but for the good of all of us. That's why we decided not to leave therapy. It was a commitment

Client: Saying what happened to me—that was the harder part, and also to tell how I was abused. It was very painful to me to talk about that—that's what was the harder part. What made me continue was that I did need help, as all of the family. I continued because I wanted to grow.

Family #5.

Aunt: I got angry because I saw it did no good for him, and for a while I wouldn't go. My husband went. Because I was angry, I missed about two, Because I saw it wasn't helping him. He was still hanging with his buddies, because my husband didn't know I went to school a couple times and saw him at lunch time, but I never told him. And one time, I went looking for him, and they couldn't find him, and I said, "Uh-huh, I ain't even going back. What for?"

Uncle: The most difficult for me was to regulate my schedule.

Family #6.

Mother: The hardest part was to set my pride aside and do things sometimes that you don't want to do, for the sake of the family. I learned how to express myself to say what I truly felt my problem was. When I got home, and I went back to the same, all that I learned in the session, I took advantage of [it], and I wanted to know more and more.

Stepfather: The most difficult was to give up my pride, especially because when I did it, my relationship got worse. And do not give up on the therapy, because it was very beneficial. Learn a lot, and I like to learn a lot. There were moments of laziness, because my relationship was getting more difficult, even-though I was behaving so well, trying to be nicer and understanding. I improved 85 percent in kindness, and my partner was not responding to that, so I felt that it doesn't make sense to change. But on the other hand, I realize that it does make sense for myself, if the relationship doesn't work. I can continue my life in better shape. I never really want to end the therapy. I wanted to leave my wife. I did not ask if the therapy could continue for me, even if my relationship ended, but in that case I would like to continue myself.

Family #7.

Client: Talk about my mother and that she used to hit me.

Younger Sister: Yes, about that.

Mother: Well, it wasn't so difficult, but there were moments that I felt bad, because she set limits to my daughters, and I told her one time," It bothers me that someone from the outside puts limits on my daughters." I felt like saying, "Leave," but I did not do it, because I thought that with all that, we were going to get to some place— something that I would feel comfortable about, because it was a lot of her words that I liked that make me react. On the other hand, I thought that my daughters were guilty about it, because when that therapist came, their behavior was bad.

Family #8.

Father: Yes, sometimes I don't have time, but I still make it. I think it was good for us. On the other hand, I did promise to go, and I should keep the promise.

Mother: Same as my husband.

Family #9.

Mother: It was difficult to me at one time. As I told you, I take an antidepressant, and there were some moments that I said to myself, "This does not make sense. I am wasting my time." Some days, I couldn't stand up from the bed. If I could not go to the session, she did home visit. Those were the difficult moments where I felt I was not improving, but the therapist did not give up on us, and she tried to accommodate us, and she was behind me. There were no excuses and no reasons not to attend my appointment. At the beginning I attended the session to look good, but after that, I wanted [to go]. In the end, I did not call her anymore, and she asked me, "Why don't you come anymore to the sessions?" And I answered, because when I was in crisis, I used to call, but I am not in crisis anymore. I acknowledged that I used to call her when we were doing bad. The therapist motivated [me] to continue.

Older Brother: Saying to each other the truth, because we did not have any type of communication before. And it was difficult, because I never did that before.

Mother: When I was depressed, I had no interest in telling my problems to anybody When you feel that someone stays there in silence—when you feel bad—that's the way I feel [about] her.

Older Brother: At the beginning, it was boring. I did not understand anything. I did not feel like going, but then I thought I needed to help me—I needed to do something.

Client: At the beginning, because I do not like to involve other people in my problems that I have in my home, and I thought, "What do I need to tell my things to people, so they feel sorry for me?" I began to see that the family was changing, that my brother began to go to school, and I thought that if he could do it, I could do it, too. My mother, my older brother, and the therapist are the ones that helped me improve in school and improve my relationship with the family.

THEME #6

Theme #6 involved thoughts/predictions about what therapy was going to be. *Theme #6A* dealt with predictions that therapy was going to be a waste of time, conflict producing, and/or worthless. Dialogue excerpts from families #1, #2, #3, # 7, and #9 follow:

Family #1.

Daughter: I didn't expect it to work, but I wanted to try.

Family #2.

Client: Bad stuff—I did not know what was going to happen.

Family #3.

Mother: I thought it wouldn't help us, that it was a loss of time, that she would leave. and we would be the same. But to the contrary, we are all together and better. We don't yell at each other anymore. We were extremely stressed before.

Client: Before we began therapy, I was always fighting with my mother. Currently we don't do that anymore. Thought therapy was going to produce conflict, but on the contrary—sometimes we fight, but not like before. We seldom fight since we ended therapy. When we do fight, then we talk about it.

Younger Sister: I thought therapy was going to help, but not so much.

Father: I also thought that it was going to be worthless, but I am very happy with it. It changed our family to good.

Family #7.

Mother: At the beginning, she saw my daughter in the school, and after that, she began to go to the house. And she said, "I had a bad impression about you because of what your daughter told me, but right now that I meet you in person, I can see how you are and I understand why are you hard on your children and that you are a good mother." I go with my daughters wherever I go.

Mother: At the beginning of the treatment, I truly thought I was going to waste my time. It bothers me to go to therapy. My life was hectic:

wake up, wake up the girls, dress them up, dress myself, go to work, go at 4:00 to pick them up. I want to do dinner—it was like a battle every day—and going to [therapy]... was like a waste of my time, one hour talking.

Family #9.

Mother: I thought I was losing my time, and I would lose my time, like one appointment or two or three boring that I would not understand anything. After a while, I began to like it; how the therapist treated my children, how all my family was changing, because my family was a mess. All were complaining. Then I began to like it more and more and more. At the beginning, when the therapist called me on the telephone, I did not like her.

Client: I thought at the beginning, when the therapist called me from the program, that it was going to be a waste of time, that it would worsen things.

Younger Brother: I thought it was going to be boring, that the therapist was going to talk about a lot of things, that they were going to ask a lot of questions.

Theme #6B dealt with family members' predictions that therapy would be helpful. Dialogue excerpts from families #1, #2, #5, #6, #8, and #9 follow:

Family #1.

Mother: I hoped it would work, that my children would listen to me.

Family #2.

Father: I did not have any negative feelings. I felt it would make us more aware of things. At the beginning, I thought maybe I did something wrong, but later, I thought about it and knew they would help explain and educate us.

Mother: No, I did not feel like we did something wrong. I did not know—I thought it was a place for help.

Family #5.

Aunt: That we needed help somewhere at the end of the line. We were having family problems, and we needed help.

Family #6.

Stepfather: When they told me about that, our relationship was very fragile, so we went to improve. We knew it was something to improve. And yes, we improved. I knew it was not going to hurt me. It depends on me. I knew who I was. I knew they were not going to put me in jail. It was to improve, and that is the way it happened.

Mother: I thought that I could learn how to communicate with my son, that he could learn stuff. I imagined things of my life and of my own mother would appear in the sessions. I thought it was going to be a process of asking questions.

Client: I thought that only my mother and me were going to assist the session; then "D" was invited, also. I thought it was going to be a one-time interview.

Family #8.

Father: I was doubtful. I was wishing it would work.

Mother: I did not know anything about it. I did not know what counseling would be about.

Family #9.

Client: On the other hand, I thought that it would be okay, because we had a lot of problems in the home—all angry every five minutes, someone fighting all the time. Because of that, I decided to give an opportunity to the program, to take everything out of our systems [so] we can feel better.

THEME #7

Theme #7 involved expressed complaints about therapy by teenagers and children. Following are dialogue excerpts from families #1, #4, #5, #6, and #7:

Family #1.

Daughter: I knew she was right, but I wanted to do it my way; the same. I was oppositional.

Family #4.

Client: When I first went to see therapist, I thought I was in trouble, because I said to myself that I had gotten into trouble. But after I got to know her, I realized that she would be a great help to me.

Family #5.

Client: For me it was like I had the mentality where I just didn't care about nothing. And it was like what would come to me; I just wouldn't care, and now I know what I think before I do certain stuff or some stuff. I still… I really don't care, so—

Client: For me it was like every time I went, I got into more trouble. It was like she was telling on me and stuff, but they didn't know whenever she would tell, so it was like whenever she would come, I would get into more trouble, so I really didn't go.

Client: I'd try and get them back, and I'd do the same thing before she took them, so it didn't really matter too much, but it helped me to get my clothes back and to do what I needed to do.

Client: In a way, I didn't really listen to her because, she wasn't anybody over me, and she didn't take care of me, so in order for me to listen to her, she had to bring in my aunt—somebody I would listen to. She had to do what she had to do.

Client: I'm like a person who stays to myself, and I don't like people trying to get in all of my business and know what I'm doing, and she kept asking me what I was doing.

Family #6.

Client: And the end—I didn't go anymore. I do not like anybody to tell me what to do, and she told me to work, and I didn't like it.

Family #7.

Client: I thought she was going to tell me when I do something wrong, why were we mean with my mother, why I was the way I was in school. At the beginning, I thought she was a mean person because she said to my mother to set consequences for our bad behavior, and that she could take things from us when we misbehaved, or time-out.

THEME #8

This theme involved family members' overall feelings and ideas regarding being all together in room with therapy. ***Theme #8A*** involved positive feelings that therapy was necessary. Following are dialogue excerpts from families #2, #3, #5, #6, #7, #8, and #9:

Family #2.

Father: Yes, it's good, because I think that counseling just the parents does not work. I think that if all of us are explained to, we can all understand better and know what each of us did wrong.

Mother: I don't have anything to say about that—but yes, it is better.

Family #3.

Mother: Because we all needed therapy—not only one. What is the point of one doing therapy and the others not—like "A"? Took therapy for one year with that doctor in psychology, and it did no good. There were no changes, because she was alone. This [therapy] gives you a good results, because we all attended those sessions.

Family #5.

Aunt: It was something we needed to do [being together in a room].

Family #6.

Mother: I felt good. My mother and my sister came to therapy with me. I wish my father would be present, but he can't. I felt very good with my sister, my mother, and my husband coming.

Client: Good. I felt it worked, especially with my problems.

Family #7.

Mother: I felt good, very good. We have no problem with my daughters going together.

Family #8.

Father: I didn't know what she wanted at the beginning. She wanted to see the whole family; therefore, we did.

Mother: The result was much better. At least we didn't fight a lot at home.

Family #9.

Younger Son: Happy, because it was helping us. I liked it when I went there.

Father: I thought it was very good. We all feel better. I was happy that everybody knew what I felt, if I felt bad.

Older Son: It was rare because we had never sat down like that. At the beginning, I felt kind of embarrassed to say what was going on in the house—who began the problems, why do we fight? And because we spelled all that out, I felt relieved.

Client: The first time I went, I did not like it. We were all there, fighting. As my mother said, it was all quarrels. But as my brother said, we had never were all together like there in the session. After a while, we began to feel more comfortable and said what we have inside, with my family members present. I was proud of my family, because we were all together and good.

Theme #8B dealt with negative feelings about therapy (e.g., arguing, disagreeing). Following are dialogue excerpts from families #1, #4, #6, and #9:

Family #1.

Mother: It was very difficult to see that my daughter would listen to someone and not to me.

Daughter: I felt nervous. I was emotional. It is hard to talk about your problems in front of the family, because we were not used to communicate with each other.

Family #4.

Mother: We argued with each other: "You do this, you do that, you shouldn't do this." She would guide us, telling us what we should do, what we should say, what we shouldn't say. If the child misbehaved, she told us how to scold him, and that if my husband was the one to scold him, how I should stay out of it, because it would not be correct if I comforted him. If the father scolds, and he comes to me, I should ask him why his father scolded him and make him see that I'm not comforting him, but showing him why he mustn't do what he did.

Client: Well, I think I felt ashamed and sad. Everyone stared at me when she walked in. "What's wrong? Why is she here?" Later on, I felt well when she came, because she helped us a lot. I felt I could speak more freely and not hold anything back.

Family #6.

Stepfather: Good. At the beginning, not so good, because we did not have a close relationship. At the end was better. At the beginning, [it] was very difficult to get connected because, as I said, the relationship was very disconnected, and it was difficult to get closer to each other. I know that we need more time—is a long process to learn how to get really close.

Family #9.

Mother: At the beginning, [when] we went to the appointments, everyone was blaming everyone: "You did this, you did that." After a while everyone began to take responsibility for their own faults, and we respond for what we did, for what we want to do. If my older son wanted to break the window, he give the idea some thought.

THEME #9

This theme involved understanding of and feelings about the problem being reframed as a family problem, rather than individual problem and understanding the link between marital dysfunction or parental well-being and behavior in children/adolescents. Following are dialogue excerpts from all families:

Family #1.

Daughter: It was not difficult to understand, because my mother is how she was—if she has no problem with me, she has it with my sister or my boyfriend. I was stubborn, myself, too. My sister was tired of being blamed for everything. I wanted to be some other place to not listen to my mother nagging.

Mother: Yes, partly because my daughters made me angry—my daughter who did not want to go to school or came late at night.

Family #2.

Mother: It's really nothing. If they come, they come. I don't blame my children or anything.

Mother: I don't think that, "Oh, it's because my children. That's why they are here"—or anything. I don't think like that at all. If I blame my children, then it's like I am unhappy for them to see us.

Family #3.

Father: I thought I was right. I always thought that—that they were all wrong—but the therapist helped me to realize that I also was guilt. I felt guilty. Even today, it is difficult, because I feel guilty for hitting my daughter. And I asked her, "Do you forgive me?" And she said, "There is nothing to forgive." The culture—and I thought [that by] hitting, they would react. I have difficulties forgiving myself. They forgive me; I do not forgive myself.

Mother: At the beginning, it was. We got all defensive, blaming each other, pointing a finger at each other, but she helped us conclude that we were all guilty. There were a lot of guilty people, not one, because she was not living alone. She was not fighting with the wall, and [the wall] was answering her. We were guilty, also, and it is hard to accept that you are mistaken. And I know I made a lot of mistakes, and in a lot [of instances] I did not. I was scared that something would happen to her, and I was trying to retain control of her and not let her be in the streets, so of course, she begin to rebel and to fight. And it made sense—I recognized I overdid it. I did not want to hurt her; I wanted to protect her. She was my doll. I was guilty —because I was the older [one], I should know how to make the rules, and I thought I was doing that. We are friends.

Family #4.

Mother: Honestly, the problem was not only my daughter's problem. It was the whole family's problem. I always felt like that, and I continue thinking in that way. She was not guilty about what happened to her. The problem was that we did not take care as we should; we realized in the therapy. The therapist pushed a lot of our issues and confronted us—what the family needed to resolve, how we can overcome obstacles.

Family #5.

Uncle: I think she was concerned about the progress of our relationship, and the only way you can note the progress is to know that people are communicating better, and it takes all of us to do that.

Uncle: It wasn't difficult for me, because I knew some things we needed straightening out, in terms of our communication. She recognized that and revealed it, and I thought it was good information to help us bring about a better understanding.

Aunt: No, it wasn't difficult for me, because I knew it was. It was more than just "D's" problem.

Client: Well, now that I think about it, it was looked at as a family problem, but I didn't feel like—I felt like it was my problem, and I'd get through it and do what I got to do to get through it. I didn't really feel that I needed her help.

Client: No. That how she [the therapist] looked at it, but I felt it was my problem.

Family #6.

Stepfather: No, it was not difficult. I knew that "S" was not the problem. I knew it, and I continue knowing it. I knew that the problem was my relationship—that we screwed up our relationship. I always knew it.

Mother: The problem was here, not "S." We made our children in the way we are. If he did not do things, [it] was because we did not told him to do it. We had a lot of problems, and that is why he was behaving in that way.

Client: It was easy for me. I did not believe it was me. I thought it was everybody's problem.

Family #7.

Mother: No, I recognized that I had a bad temper, that for me it is difficult to control myself, because when I get awful mad, nobody can control me. I knew it would be difficult for someone to help me change. She helped me understand that, if we want and make the effort, we can achieve all that we want. All is about having the strength to do it. If you want to change, you can do it; if you don't want to, you will stay in the same place.

Family #8.

Father: I agree the problem is related to the entire family.

Family #9.

Mother: Because she saw that the problem was not only my daughter, that it was a family problem. The therapist used to say, "The problem is not your daughter—it is yourself, and if you are doing bad, they are all going to perform in the same way. And it happened that the first time that I stopped and worked out my own stuff, everyone began to put themselves together. Was depressed—all of them were depressed. I was out of control; they began to be out of control. The therapist explained to me that my daughter was not the guilty one, that if I wanted them to be okay, I should work on being okay myself.

THEME #10

This theme involved insights, feelings that participants expressed about their family of origin, insight about the multigenerational transmission process, and participation of many family members in the sessions. Following are dialogue excerpts from families #1, #3, #4, #5, #6, and #7:

Family #1.

Daughter: One time she [the therapist] explained to me how my mother feels. The therapist told me that my mother acted like this because of my mother's childhood history. She was hurt a lot of times and mistreated, and she wants the best for us for our future, because she did not have a good one, so she wanted a good future for us.

Family #3.

Mother: She took me back to my childhood and helped me process my traumas. She helped me in confronting problems that I was not willing to confront. She helped me a lot. I felt a lot of support from her. She helped me to mature. I felt a lot of support.

Father: It really helped me a lot. I was very attached to my mother, and she [the therapist] helped me to rethink that first it was my own family, my children, and my wife—that I shouldn't be thinking all the time about my mother.

Family #4.

Mother: Here we learn that you need to think about yourself first, yourself second, and yourself third, even if it sounds selfish. First is your own family and yourself. Outside the door, it doesn't matter. That is something we learn from the therapist: that we need to protect the inside, and the outside doesn't matter. The most important are your family. Even my family of origin is less important.

Family #5.

Uncle: Well, I think one of the things she started talking about was family values in our past history with my father and mother and my wife's father and mother and it helped to bring about a better understanding of what we do, what we don't.

Aunt: I think it's called a family tree.

Family #6.

Mother: Well, I am affected by my family of origin, so the more she knows my family, the more she can know who I am, why I behave the way I behave. She wanted them to also talk about me and help me with my problems.

Client: Because of how my mother said the problems began with my grandmother.

Mother: That my mother came to therapy helped me a lot.

Family #7.

Mother: Yes, she understood, since she began to ask me about my childhood and gave me feedback. I thought she perfectly understood me.

THEME #11

This theme concerned what participants would do about future problems after therapy ended. **Theme #11A** dealt with family members who would try to resolve problems by themselves.

Following are dialogue excerpts from families #3, #4, #5, #6, #8, and #9:

Family #3.

Father: Communication, so we don't repeat.

Mother: Talking, with communication.

Client: Talking a lot, but nothing would happen again—I am one hundred percent sure.

Mother: When "A" gets mad, I say, "Leave her alone. It's going to be over."

Father: When she gets stubborn, I ignore her. I don't get mad. I take it like a joke. I need to be calm, and everything will get back to normal.

Family #4.

Mother: I would talk about it, I would talk about the problem we have. We all give opinions, and we come to the conclusion, and you resolve it.

Client: I talk to my parents, and I look for help with them.

Mother: It was very good, the program I would like to continue growing as a family. My daughter is all changed. She has not had any problems in school. She made a drastic change—a very good one.

Family #5.

Client: For me, I really didn't like therapy, so therapy wouldn't be my first choice. Say if I had a problem with someone, I would go to that person, and if we can't resolve it, then—

Client: I would talk to somebody who respects me that I can just talk to, and they would just listen until I get it all off my chest and feel good.

Family #6.

Stepfather: I think I would try to resolve the problem. It is difficult because I improve a lot in my behavior, and my wife, a lot of times, is mad and does not want to talk.

Mother: I would try to find a solution. If I love him, I would not leave him. I would intend to understand the person. I would try to talk and negotiate, because I had difficulties in the area. We had a lot of problems. I continue fighting against these difficulties I have, because I love my husband, because a divorce would be very painful for us and the kids.

Client: I need to continue improving my grades and continue communicating with "D."

Family #8.

Father: I will try to solve the problem by myself first.

Family #9.

Mother: I would use the techniques I learned with my therapist to try to resolve the problems. If I got depressed, I will go to the doctor. If I see that my children had problems, I will ask for help. If my husband begins to drink again, I will hospitalize him. Before, I couldn't make a decision for these type of problems. I never made up my mind. I learned from my therapist to do everything in the right time.

Theme #11B dealt with family members asking for some kind of treatment or help for a problem. Following are dialogue excerpts from families #1, #2, #4, #5, #7, #8, and #9:

Family #1.

Mother: I don't know. Maybe I would call the police other program again.

Daughter: I don't know, because the therapist no longer works in the program. Maybe I would call program again.

Family #2.

Mother: If there comes a time when my children don't listen or behave, we will ask them to help again. It helps us understand more—learn more and see things differently.

Father: If they see and feel there is a need for another family member for treatment, we welcome that. We see it—that it will help us to be a better family to one another.

Family #4.

Mother: I would like to continue with the therapy because one learns something every day. Small incidents appear unexpectedly, and you have to cope with them. She helps you in resolving them.

Family #5.

Uncle: Go to Camp A—it's a Christian camp up in northern California. They have a wonderful therapist up there who deals with family problems and issues about how to make family life better.

Uncle: No. Faith and belief were something that was missing in the whole part of our counseling. I think that's a helpful element to—well, actually I believe in the prayer life of the individual. I believe it can help people change their attitudes and aspirations when they pray about it and ask God for direction. I'm a Bible believer. In Proverbs, chapter 3 verse 5: "In all thy ways acknowledge him, and he shall rectify."

Family #7.

Mother: I would try to go to counseling with the same therapist. She really helped me. She helped me a lot.

Family #8.

Father: If I can't solve the problem, then I will seek help.

Mother: If it happened again, it would be very bad, but I would put my daughter in a group home.

Family #9.

> Client: First, I would try to do as the therapist used to say, and if not, I would get into the program again.

THEME #12

This theme involved family members' opinions, feelings, and concepts about the therapist. ***Theme #12A*** concerned family members who felt that the therapist helped them to see what they were doing right and wrong. Following are dialogue excerpts from families #1, #3, #4, and #5:

Family #1.

> Daughter: She affects the entire family. She taught us things, what is right or wrong. She gave us good advice, but we have difficulties following through, because it is hard in my family to communicate. Lately, it is better, because I understand more.

Family #3.

> Client: It helped me, because she pointed things out to me that I was doing wrong.

> Father: I thought I was right. I always thought that—that they were all wrong—but the therapist helped me to realize that I also was guilt. I felt guilty. Even today it is difficult, because I feel guilty for hitting my daughter. And I asked her, "Do you forgive me?" And she said, "There is nothing to forgive." The culture—and I

thought [that by] hitting, they would react. I have difficulties forgiving myself. They forgive me; I do not forgive myself.

Father: She made me see my errors, that I was wrong.

Mother: She helped us to improve, showing us our problems and to understand what we were doing wrong and what we were doing good, and little by little she explained to us. And I don't know how she left—treatment ended, and we were in a much better position, and we continued like that. We also had relationship problems, and those she also helped us overcome.

Family #4.

Client: She helped me see what's right and what's wrong. It helped me in getting along with my family, how to express myself. If they trust you, why shouldn't you trust them?

Client: For me what the therapist did, even if I am repeating myself, she helped me to overcome what was right or wrong—that you had a commitment—that you needed to perform as you committed. She wrote on a paper our agreements, and if we did not follow through, she showed us the paper. She gave us a time frame. She helped us a lot.

Family #5.

Uncle: For me, it was reaffirming what I always teach in terms of being truthful and honest. I got to be honest with you—you appreciate the value, even if sometimes it might be frightful or against what you actually believe in, but learn to appreciate that.

Aunt: And see, he broke his contract. That's why she took them the last time, because he didn't keep his word on the contract, and he thought she was just going to let it go, but no, she did not. He thought she probably forgot about. No, no, no—and she was right. Once you sign a contract, you're not supposed to break the contract. That's what it is.

Aunt: Right, because she took them twice, and the first time he was still out there, but the second time, I think it was more hurtful because he didn't think she was really going to do it the second time, and also she made him sign a contract, too. And remember, you didn't keep your word on the contract, you see. Remember she made you do that?

Theme #12B dealt with the concept that the therapist displayed warmth, empathy, self-disclosure, and trustworthiness, and treated participants as equals. Following are dialogue excerpts from families #2, #3, #7, and #9:

Family #2.

Mother: They have a warm heart toward us. I believe in them when they explained things to us.

Father: They are happy and joyful when they come, just like you. When you come, you talk, laugh, and we laugh together. It makes us very happy. Like if you look unhappy and mad, both of us are not happy. When they come, I'm comfortable and always [asking] questions and very blunt about it, if I don't understand something.

Father: She said she had four or five siblings, too. Sometimes they have conflicts, get mad at each other. The younger one feels like the parents don't ask all the children to do chores, and the parents only love one; the others the parents don't love. She said like that.

Family #3.

Mother: Some therapists try to demonstrate that they are superior to you, and this therapist showed us that we were equal, and she built trust with us.

Client: She never said your mother told me this or that. She took the truth from me. I used to say, "You know, I did this." She did not breach confidentiality. I knew that if I told her something secret, she would not tell that.

Family #7.

Mother: But after a while I began to like it. I began to like her coming. She was like a confidante—someone to spell all out. She really helped me a lot.

Mother: With time passing by, I think the therapist cared about us, and everything changed. She tried to talk with me and with the girls. She made me feel good.

Family #9.

Mother: And I trust her, because she followed our secrecy policy. She was a good therapist, like a sister—I trusted her, and I have affection toward her. We all have good experiences.

Client: We talked alone in some sessions. I spelled all out, because I trust her, when she said that she would keep the stuff confident. She did it. She helped realize how important it is to have the family in good terms, and not a depressive family like before. She helped me to appreciate my family and my brothers, and also the school and the importance of education. Before, it did not matter to me have good grades or have a degree. I realize that a lot of children in this world don't have the opportunity of going to the school for free, and that I need to take advantage of this. She also helped me to appreciate my family.

Client: I think she understood us. She used to tell us that she was like me when she was a child. I felt like she was an older sister. I think she understood me very well.

Theme #12C dealt with the concept that the therapist was like an expert, teacher, medical doctor, and/mediator, and that she helped participants bring order to their homes and gave advice. Following are dialogue excerpts from families #1through #6:

Family #1.

Daughter: There have been many things that are very helpful. But I just don't want to accept the fact that the advice she gave me was good for me.

Family #2.

Father: Who they want to see or who they want to get to know? It's okay. They came to teach the children and to do the right thing.

Family #3.

Client: She is like a teacher—someone with whom I could exchange opinions.

Mother: It was hard, but good, because when you look for help and you find [someone] who can help you, it is good. You can't get along with whatever person—it needs to be a real professional, who studied for that and has a degree and because of that, the therapist really helped us.

Mother: She came and confronted all of us together. At the beginning, we met at school, and after that, she came to the home. At the beginning, she saw "A" alone, and then the whole family. Little by little, she put all of us together.

Family #4.

Mother: Because she is a therapist, she studies and sees the case, through her experience, like a medical doctor. Honestly, she understood us, and she has a very good memory. She never forgot what happened in the last session, or fifteen days before we saw each other. We came, and she asked us questions like what happened, what had we done during those two weeks that we did not see each other.

Client: I think she saw the problems differently, because she has more experience and she knows more about life, because she studied for that.

Family #5.

Aunt: And she knows her job, and she does her job well. It didn't matter who she threw the punch at, she threw it, and that's the way it should be. She didn't take no sides on either one of us.

Family #6.

Stepfather: I think she did her job, what she was supposed to do. She said some truth. She gave us some ideas that she has of how to resolve problems, therapist have ideals of how a healthy family should be. She gave to things the importance that [they] should have, and the result, as I told you, was that we are together right now.

Theme #12D dealt with the concept that the therapist saw the reality of the situation and confronted the participants. The therapist was active, strong, determined in pushing, and inspired respect. Following are dialogue excerpts from families #3, #4, #5, #7, and #9:

Family #3.

Client: I used to talk a lot with the therapist. Sometimes I was angry at her, because she was too direct, and she told me things upfront, and I used to argue with her.

Mother: She came and confronted all of us together. At the beginning, we met at school, and after that she came to the home. At the beginning she saw "A" alone, and then the whole family. Little by little, she put all of us together.

Family #4.

Mother: It was an important confrontation that we had. Neither my husband nor the therapist gave up.

Family #5.

Aunt: I think we really continued because she was really determined, and if someone is determined to do something, and you know that it's a good program, then you hang in there and do it, even though my husband has a busy schedule, and I know he was busy being a pastor and a community leader, because we would always try to find time around his time. I guess I would look forward to seeing her.

Uncle: But I thought she handled—she a very good counselor who did not compromise on either side—who was very thorough. I think it was really good on her part to be persistent at getting people together. She really was right on about that.

Family #7.

Mother: I think she did. I think she had presence. She can say things, do things, and resolve disagreements that can hurt, and then you are happy again.

Family #9.

Father: The therapist made me nervous, because she said that if I didn't stop drinking, I was going to end up in a rehab center, and because it is bad example for my children. That is true. There was a moment that I was drinking and drinking, and she was putting pressure on me to stop.

Mother: But she insisted so much that she gave me curiosity. She gave me trust that something good was going to happen, and everybody changed, because my son was doing very bad—my son goes to school right now and works.

Mother: He was scared and had respect for the therapist. At the beginning I used to say to him—"I will tell the therapist what you did," and he did not do it. The therapist used to tell me, "Use me. Use my name if you need—if your family is calm, that is okay."

Mother: The therapist used to call me before the session and said, "I am waiting for you. If you don't come, I go to your house." The therapist used to call me before the session and said, "Our appointment is in ten minutes. I am waiting for you. Come fast—if not, I can go to your home."

Father: The therapist used to say, "Go and find a job, so you will have less problems in your head." I am lucky I find a job. I did not work for ten years. She used to say, "Work." I really appreciate the therapist.

Mother: She has a lot of courage; she confronts us; she is very expressive. This is true.

THEME #13

This theme involved setting boundaries. Following are dialogue excerpts from families #2, #3, #4, #5, and #8:

Family #2.

Father: She said to give chores to all the children in the same amount. Like "S"—he does most of the things himself—we didn't ask him to. We are afraid that she thinks we ask "S" to do too many chores. We didn't ask him, but [he] thought about it himself. Like toward the end of the month, "S" would bake and cook—cake and other things. When he finished, he would share with all the siblings.

Family #3.

Client: I saw her as someone who put limits on me.

Mother: We ended therapy one year ago. Before, if someone did something wrong, we went to her and complained. We pointed a finger at her, so she could set limits.

Family #4.

Client: She also made us get closer—that my father and mother needed to sleep together, with the baby outside their bed.

Mother: To put limits because I did not know how to set them, to learn to set boundaries.

Mother: It helped me. It helped the entire family. I learned to believe in my children, to set limits.

Mother: She made changes around in our family: how we should organize ourselves as a family. She showed me how to share the same household with my daughter, because I have lived with my daughter for a short amount of time. And how to live with my husband—to chat more, to share more with him. We still have a long way to go—have our own private space. But we'll get there, little by little.

Mother: Because we all need the therapy. We need to know the opinion of all of us. She did not want to "triangle."

Family #5.

Uncle: Do you remember other things that she did? Well, that stood out —but she did so much, because I remember her taking his clothes when he would not do what he was supposed to do. Every time he didn't do what he was supposed to do, she would take away his clothes, and well, that was a hurtful thing, because he loved looking good. That was the only thing he could get was his clothes.

Aunt: Everything she did, I think, was helpful, because like I said, the first time she took his clothes, that was helpful, because he kept doing what he wanted to do, because he would not believe it. He did not believe she was going to do it a second time. All of it was helpful, because if she had not done all the things she did do, he wouldn't have marched [graduated].

Client: The advice of the therapist, the limits, and the patience she had with us—the things she said.

Family #9.

Mother: Even with the baby, she set boundaries. She used to show me how to treat the baby.

Client: She put rules in the house, so there would be consequences in case we misbehave. The most important was to spell all out, all of us, we were all the time in a bad mood, and we were fighting. Think that is what happened, and that is why the family changed.

Client: The advice of the therapist, the limits, and the patience she had with us—the things she said.

THEME #14

This theme involved issues of culture and language. Following are dialogue excerpts from families #1, #2, #3, #4, and #7:

Family #1.

Mother: The language barrier was a problem.

Family #2.

Mother: She wanted to know and understand about [southeast Asian] traditions, and culture, too.

Client: I think she helped us, like a family, all together. I had been going to therapy with another one, and she did not help me in anything. I attend those sessions for one year and a half, and it did not help me at all, because that woman did not speak Spanish, and she couldn't understand the rest of us. My parents were absolutely out of the treatment. I tried to change, but they couldn't realize [the change]. That person help me with nothing, nothing—but this therapist for this program; she helped us all together, and she helped us a lot.

Family #3.

Client: The therapist helped me to understand that a lot of things were cultural, like hitting. That is the way they deal with children in Latin America, and I understood my father. She really helped us when she put all of us together, and each of us separate, also.

Family #4.

Mother: She gave us examples, how do we need to behave? Because here is another culture—is a different type of life.

Mother: She did not see the things different, because she also came from the south. She had experience working with families from Latin America and America that are almost the same. Here, the families are different than Latino-American families. She had studied how to work with families in different types of situations and experience than she had. She saw the problems more.

Family #7.

Mother: We took this program in the school of my daughter, where we worked with two therapists. With the first one, we had some communication problems, because we do not speak English, and then they referred us to the therapist with whom we worked. With her we had better communication, and we worked with her until three weeks ago. For us, she was a good therapist and a good person.

THEME #15

This theme involved participants' feelings and perceptions regarding how well the therapist understood the family's problem(s). Following are dialogue excerpts from families #1, #2, #3, #4, #6, #7, #8, and #9:

Family #1.

Mother: She understands that I am worried.

Daughter: She understands me most of the time. Sometimes I did not open up myself, so she can't help me.

Family #2.

Father: They did not assume. They understood everything. I tell you the truth. They analyzed the case and learned the problem.

Family #3.

Mother: I believe that, yes. And she talked with each of us alone, and she saw the problem—that my husband was very sensitive and too aggressive, that my daughter was very spoiled, and her sister, too—and a lot of things she began to notice that helped us. She confronted each of us, and she realized the problem: that we all loved each other very much, but we lacked problem-solving skills. She understood that. We live in a country where there are a lot of problems, and we did not know how to take care of our daughter so that nothing happened to her. We did not know how until she taught us how.

Family #4.

Mother: Because she is a therapist, she studies and sees the case, through her experience, like a medical doctor. Honestly, she understood us, and she has a very good memory. She never forgot what happened in the last session or fifteen days before we saw each other. We came, and she asked us questions, like what happened, what had we done during those two weeks that we did not see each other.

Client: She understood me, because she gave me advice—how to improve what I did wrong. I believe the therapist really understood me.

Family #6.

Stepfather: I think she saw the problems as they are, because both myself, and "P" showed the true self to her. I think that this is a long process that I wish it would continue, but was very good. I believe she understood us.

Family #7.

Mother: Yes, she understood, since she began to ask me about my childhood and gave me feedback. I thought she perfectly understood me.

Family #8.

Mother: Yes, I think she understood our problems completely. Every time I told her about our problems, she seemed to understand it very well.

Family #9.

Older Son: I felt the therapist was with me. She understood what I said, compared with my ex-therapist, who used to yell at me. I did not understand that woman; she had a strange accent, while the therapist of this program— we understood each other very well. When I explained something, she advised me—she listened to me.

Older Brother: I think the therapist understood us.

Client: I think she understood us. She used to tell us that she was like me when she was a child. I felt like she was an older sister. I think she understood me very well.

EXAMPLE OF SOME INTERVIEWS

QUESTIONS TO INTERVIEWEES

1. *If another family came to you and said, "We are going to go to the program to do what you did"; could you explain what it would be like?*

2. *What did you expect would happen in the program before you went there?*

3. *What was it like for you to bring your whole family to therapy?*

4. *Can you describe what happened in therapy? What was it like for each of you?*

5. *Tell me about your therapist and what she did?*

6. *Why do you think that your therapist wanted to see all the members of the family participating in the process?*

7. *What was the most difficult part of therapy, and what made you continue?*

8. *What do you think was helpful in therapy? Describe it and explain why.*

9. *In what ways did the therapist see your problems in a different way than you did?*

10. How well did your therapist understand you and your problems?

11. Did you change the way you viewed your problem at the end of therapy?

12. Do you remember a time in particular that was significant as the starting point for resolving your problems?

13. Do you remember a moment that you felt like quitting therapy? If so, what made you continue?

14. Was it difficult for you to accept the fact that the problem was not your son/daughter's problem, but the entire family's problem?

15. If you had the same or a different problem again, what would you do?

Examples of interviews after treatment has ended with three therapists: one Latin-American, one American, and one European.

FAMILY #1 ASIAN FAMILY

CAUCASIAN, MASTER-LEVEL THERAPIST
therapist supervised by Dr.Cabouli

Transcription

INTERVIEWER: **If another family came to you and said, we are going to the program to do what you did"; could you explain what it would be like?**

MOTHER: Yes, I would tell them.

DAUGHTER: Yes.

INTERVIEWER: **What did you expect would happen in the program before you went there?**

DAUGHTER: I didn't expect it to work, but I wanted to try.

MOTHER: I hoped it would work.

INTERVIEWER: **What was it like for you to bring your whole family to therapy?**

MOTHER: I felt better. It was very difficult.

DAUGHTER: I felt nervous. I was emotional… [unintelligible]

INTERVIEWER: **Can you describe what happened in therapy? What was it like for each of you?**

MOTHER: It helps both of us to communicate.

DAUGHTER: It helps me to understand my mother better.

INTERVIEWER: **Tell me about your therapist and what she did.**

DAUGHTER: She affects the entire family.

MOTHER: She helps me to understand the responsibility of an eighteen-year-old.

INTERVIEWER: **Why do you think that your therapist wanted to see all the members of the family participating in the process?**

MOTHER: I don't know.

DAUGHTER: I think it is good for us.

INTERVIEWER: **What was the most difficult part of therapy, and what made you continue?**

MOTHER: When brother was rebelling or disobeying me, the therapist helps me to understand why that was.

DAUGHTER: When we don't know how to help ourselves, and we want to avoid the problem. But we knew we needed help.

INTERVIEWER: **What do you think was helpful in therapy? Describe it and explain why.**

MOTHER: I understand that I am too concerned about my daughter. I should relax, but it was very difficult not to be concerned about my daughter.

DAUGHTER: There have been many things that are very helpful. But I just don't want to accept the fact... [unintelligible]

INTERVIEWER: **In what ways did your therapist understand you and your problems?**

MOTHER: She understands that I am worried.

DAUGHTER: She understands me most of the time.

INTERVIEWER: **How well did your therapist understand you and your problems?**

DAUGHTER: She understands my problems very well.

INTERVIEWER: **Did you change the way you viewed your problem at the end of the therapy?**

DAUGHTER: The therapist made me change sometimes for the better, sometimes for the worse.

MOTHER: Yes.

INTERVIEWER: **Do you remember a time in particular that was significant as the starting point for resolving your problems?**

DAUGHTER: One time, she [the therapist] explained to me how my mother feels.

MOTHER: I don't remember.

INTERVIEWER: **Do you remember a moment that you felt like quitting therapy? If so, what made you continue?**

DAUGHTER: Yes. My mother was so stubborn.

MOTHER: Lately.

INTERVIEWER: **Was it difficult for you to accept the fact that the problem was not your daughter's problem, but the entire family's problem?**

MOTHER: Yes.

DAUGHTER: Yes.

INTERVIEWER: **If you had the same or a different problem again, what would you do?**

MOTHER: I don't know. Maybe I would call the police or a therapist.

DAUGHTER: I don't know, because the therapist no longer works the agency. Maybe I would call agency again.

FAMILY #5: AFRICAN AMERICAN CLIENT

Therapist: Dr.Cabouli

Transcription

INTERVIEWER: **If another family came to you and said, "We are going to the program to do what you did," could you explain what it would be like?**

UNCLE: Yes, it's a program to determine how a family can better communicate or get a clearer understanding between the family members to bring them closer together.

AUNT: About the same thing.

CLIENT: I mean, it was good she came to help some. I guess it's a good thing.

INTERVIEWER: **Okay, number two: There are not right or wrong answers, so speak freely. What did you expect would happen in the program before you went there? Before you ever got to therapy, what was going through your mind? What were you thinking?**

AUNT: That we needed help somewhere at the end of the line. We were having family problems, and we needed help.

INTERVIEWER: **So what did you expect would happen in the program before you went?**

AUNT: That means I would know how to deal with the family issues that were oppressing me at the time.

UNCLE: I thought it was to bring about better communication among our family to help us really understand each other. We might have been saying the same things, but we needed a mediator.

CLIENT: For me, it was like I had the mentality where I just didn't care about nothing. And it was like what would come to me, I just wouldn't care, and now I know what I think before I do certain stuff or some stuff. I still… [unintelligible] where I really don't care, so…

MOTHER: Can you turn the TV down some? You caught yourself.

INTERVIEWER: **What was it like for you to bring your whole family to therapy?**

AUNT: It was something we needed to do.

INTERVIEWER: **Did you have any reservations?**

AUNT: Nope.

UNCLE: Not for me, either

AUNT: I'm the one who asked for it.

INTERVIEWER: **Can you describe what happened in therapy? What was it like for each of you?**

M: For me, it made me check myself out, and it also made me realize some of the points I wasn't aware of, and it also helped me to have a better relationship with my husband, and it also helped me to have a better relationship. [Relationships] tend to break, because these days, these young people, it's hard [for them] to understand you.

CLIENT: For me, it was like, every time I went, I got into more trouble. It was like she was telling on me and stuff, but they didn't know whenever she would tell, so it was like whenever she would come, I would get into more trouble, so I really didn't go.

M: Also, I want to say, too, that if she hadn't come, I don't know if he would have really graduated, because it made us see a lot of what he needed to do to go in the right direction, because he was going in the wrong direction with his peers.

INTERVIEWER: **You graduated?**

AUNT: Uh huh.

INTERVIEWER: **Congratulations!**

AUNT: Thanks God!

INTERVIEWER: **That's fantastic!**

UNCLE: But I thought she handled…a very, uh, good counselor who did not compromise on either side…who was very thorough. I think it was really good on her part to be persistent at getting people together. She really was right on about that.

AUNT: And she knows her job, and she does her job well. It didn't matter who she threw the punch at, she threw it, and that's the way it should be. She didn't take no sides on either one of us.

INTERVIEWER: **What was that like for you…no compromise?**

UNCLE: For me, it was reaffirming what I always teach in terms of being truthful and honest. I got to be honest with you…you appreciate the value, even if sometimes it might be frightful or against what you actually believe in, but learn to appreciate that.

INTERVIEWER: **Tell me about your therapist and what she did. Maybe you could tell more about what she did and the process of therapy. What was really going on? What was she doing? How did she do it?**

UNCLE: Well, I think one of the things she started talking about was family values in our past; history with my father and mother and my wife's father and mother; and helped to bring about a better understanding of what we do, what we don't.

AUNT: I think it's called a family tree.

UNCLE: Do you remember other things that she did? Well, that stood out…but she did so much, because I remember her taking his clothes when he would not do what he was supposed to do. Every time he didn't do what he was supposed to do, she would take away his clothes, and well, that was a hurtful thing because, he loved looking good. That was the only thing he could get was his clothes.

INTERVIEWER: **Anything from you for that question? What the process was like, or if you can describe what she did?**

M: Well, tell her now you felt when she took your clothes, because she took them twice.

CLIENT: Well, taking my clothes was the only thing that bothered me, but other than that, it didn't matter.

INTERVIEWER: **So it mattered in what way?**

CLIENT: I'd try and get them back, and I'd do the same thing before she took them, so it didn't really matter too much, but it helped me to get my clothes back and to do what I needed to do.

INTERVIEWER: **At first it didn't matter.**

AUNT: Right, because she took them twice, and the first time he was still out there, but the second time, I think it was more hurtful, because he didn't think she was really going to do it the second time, and also, she made him sign a contract, too. And remember, you didn't keep your word on the contract, you see. Remember she made you do that?

INTERVIEWER: **So contracts, family trees, taking clothes...those are very descriptive.**

AUNT: And see, he broke his contract. That's why she took them the last time, because he didn't keep his word on the contract, and he thought she was just going to let it go, but no, she did not. He thought she probably forgot about. No, no, no…and she was right. Once you sign a contract, you're not supposed to break the contract. That's what it is.

INTERVIEWER: **Do you want to add anything to that? No? Okay, number six. Why do you think that your therapist wanted to see all the members of the family participating in the process?**

AUNT: Well, that's the only way it'll work, unless the whole family participates. One can't do it by himself. Have to be a team.

UNCLE: I think she was concerned about the progress of our relationship, and the only way you can note the progress is to know that people are communicating better, and it takes all of us to do that.

INTERVIEWER: **And why do you think she brought in the whole family? What do you think she was thinking?**

CLIENT: In a way, I didn't really listen to her because she wasn't anybody over me, and she didn't take care of me, so in order for me to listen to her, she had to bring in my aunt C, somebody I would listen to. She had to do what she had to do.

INTERVIEWER: **Interesting. Okay, number seven. What was the most difficult part of therapy, and what made you continue?**

UNCLE: The most difficult for me was to regulate my schedule.

INTERVIEWER: **Ha, I hear you.**

AUNT: I think we really continued because she was really determined, and if someone is determined to do something, and you know that it's a good program, then you hang in there and do it, even though my husband has a busy schedule, and I know he was busy being a pastor and a community leader, because we would always try to find time around his time. I guess I would look forward to seeing her.

INTERVIEWER: **So you don't remember a time that was difficult for you?**

AUNT: Not really, because even sometimes I would have to take my daycare kids with me.

INTERVIEWER: **Okay. And for you, what was the most difficult part of therapy for you?**

CLIENT: Like I said, it was when she took my clothes. And me wanting to continue? I wanted to quit a long time ago.

INTERVIEWER: **What made you continue?**

CLIENT: She would come here, because she would send passes at school, and I wouldn't even go. So she would come to the house, and that's the only way she would see me.

AUNT: Well, see, we didn't even know that she would send passes, and he wouldn't even go, because she never told us that. She wouldn't tell on him. He thought she was squealing, but she was not. She never told us, but if it were me, I would have gone to every room and gotten him. So that's the difference between her and me. When he would've seen me coming to the door, he would've been ashamed and gotten on up. She never did tell, did she, babe? And see, he thought she was telling on him, but she did not. Even when I knew that he was running with the wrong crowd, she never told us he was running with the wrong crowd. See, most of his peers told us at school. His peers and some of his teachers told us when I'd go to the school.

INTERVIEWER: **What do you think was helpful in therapy?**

AUNT: Everything she did, I think, was helpful, because like I said, the first time she took his clothes, that was helpful because he kept doing what he wanted to do because he would not believe it. He did not believe she was going to do it a second time. All of it was helpful, because if she had not done all the things she did do, he wouldn't have marched [graduated].

CLIENT: I had to pass my senior exhibition, regardless.

AUNT: No, no, no. First of all, you had to turn around. You were on the wrong track. You were hanging, remember? From doing right. You had to turn around, first.

INTERVIEWER: **What do you think was helpful for you in therapy personally?**

AUNT: Finding out different points about myself. What I needed to do to better my relationship…even myself.

INTERVIEWER: **Can you give me an example?**

AUNT: Yes. I used to talk real, real loud. I don't talk loud as I used to any more, so that stood out, and she showed me, and she was saying, like my husband always told me, too, You're going to have a heart attack getting excited and stuff." And I think I saw that, and that stood out more than all that stuff.

INTERVIEWER: **And for yourself, what was helpful in therapy?**

UNCLE: The fact of getting together and communicating the matter that we need to better understand each other and listen to each other.

INTERVIEWER: **Did you feel that you were listened to more, or that you were able to listen to what other people were having to say more?**

UNCLE: Right, I was able to listen to what other people had to say more. That's one of the key elements in really getting better communication, as you know. You have to be willing to listen. Most people don't listen. They want to spot me out whenever they feel an opening. They're not willing to sit back and be relaxed and take their turn and say whatever they need to say.

INTERVIEWER: **Good input. You're up to bat. What was helpful in therapy for you?**

CLIENT: The good things…I guess she's saying it helped me get through school and helped me focus, but I didn't really like it, so…

INTERVIEWER: **What didn't you like?**

CLIENT: I'm like a person who stays to myself, and I don't like people trying to get in all of my business and know what I'm doing, and she kept asking me what I was doing.

AUNT: You know, he may be right, because when I had to meet his teachers at parents' night, they said, "Hi, Mrs. B…" I said, "No, I'm Mrs. M…" So they said, "Oh, you're not D's mom?" So I said, "No, I'm his aunt. His mother's deceased." Then D said, "Don't be telling nobody my mother's dead." I said, "If someone asks me something, I can't lie."

CLIENT: But it's none of their business.

AUNT: If they ask, I can't lie. His mother been gone for ten years. If somebody asks, I have to tell the truth. It's different if they didn't ask, but they asked. Lord have mercy. Somewhere at the end of the line, like he said. They're in his business, but that's not being in his business. They just didn't know. We were wanting to know why he didn't want no one to know that his mom was dead, because she's been dead for ten years. At first, I thought he had accepted it, but now he's saying they're in his business.

INTERVIEWER: **So, going to question nine. Just remember, I'm not doing therapy, so if I'm not responding or giving you lots of feedback, it's because I'm trying to be as neutral as possible and letting you give it all. In what ways did the therapist see your problems in a different way than you did?**

AUNT: I don't think she was there to see our problems the same way. She was there to find how we could solve our problems.

INTERVIEWER: **How did she see your problem?**

UNCLE: Actually, she realized we weren't being open in our communication. We'd hold back. I know I would. I would hold back and not verbalize how I felt, because I did not want to further irritate the feeling in our conversation. And I'm still that way. I let people talk. I learn more when other people talk, and I listen. It helps me to understand what I need to do in order to help solve their problems. Not for them…with them.

INTERVIEWER: **So I think you're saying she saw your problems as not being able to talk or express…**

UNCLE: Yes, nonverbal.

INTERVIEWER: **Okay, so did you see that as a problem, because, the question says, "In what ways did the therapist see your problem in a different way than you saw your problem?"**

UNCLE: Yeah, I saw that as a problem from the start?

INTERVIEWER: **Any areas of disagreement on how you saw the problem?**

AUNT: Why, sure, there were time when we had disagreements about the problem. What do you think, D?

CLIENT: She said my problems were my grades at school, but I didn't see any problem with that. I felt I had that all under control, which I did; but I guess she felt she stepped in and solved that or whatever, but I felt I had it all taken care of.

INTERVIEWER: **What did help you, then, because I know you did say you felt you were helped? Is there anything that was helpful that hasn't been said so far that really was helpful that wasn't about the grades? Something we're missing?**

CLIENT: The only thing that probably really helped me and kept me focused was I knew I had to get my clothes back. I wanted my clothes, so I had to focus at school. That's about the only thing that really helped me was taking away my clothes.

INTERVIEWER: **How well did your therapist understand you and your problems?**

UNCLE: I think it was very clear that we didn't have open communication like we should.

AUNT: He said it right.

INTERVIEWER: **Did she understand your problems well?**

CLIENT: Well, me, I really didn't think that I had a problem. She would see a problem that I guess she wanted me to work on, but I didn't really see that I had any problems.

INTERVIEWER: **Did you change the way you viewed your problem by the end of therapy?**

UNCLE: I guess, to some degree, I did, because we had made an agreement that I would be responsible to be the lead person in helping D to correct his attitude. But by the end of...well, my wife usually would, without me agreeing, she would just take over anyway. I think it was helpful to me to understand that she was going to do that, whether I agreed to it or not. We agreed that I would handle the problem, but at the very end, even though we agreed, my wife was coming in and still taking over.

INTERVIEWER: **How did you feel about that?**

UNCLE: Well, I just felt like I was going to opt out and not say anything, so I ended up being silent again.

INTERVIEWER: **Okay, so you, at first, had an idea that you would be more in control, really active in changing the problem, and then you found your wife to be managing that more.**

UNCLE: Right, yes.

INTERVIEWER: **How about you? Did you change the way you viewed your problem by the end of therapy?**

AUNT: I thought I did, but my husband said I didn't, so I don't know, because I thought sometimes I would and sometimes...

UNCLE: Let D answer that.

CLIENT: Depends on...I guess I don't even know what my problem was. For me, it was like, if something got in my way, I'd just try to go around it, or I'd just brush it off and keep going. I really didn't feel that I had a problem.

AUNT: He has to remember that D used to play both of us, and I know that. He would play me against him and him against me.

INTERVIEWER: **So did any of that change by the end of therapy?**

AUNT: 'Cause I realized that. He was always coming to me asking can he do this, can he do that, and I'd say, "You know, you're supposed to be asking Papa." I had to really realize all of this. But I guess that's normal for kids to do that…play one against the other. I can understand if he asked me, and Papa wasn't here, but he'd come in while papa was sitting right here.

INTERVIEWER **So that's a really good issue, actually; so actually, it wasn't a problem you were even aware of, and you became more aware?**

AUNT: As it went on, that he was playing one against the other. And sometimes I knew. I never said this to my husband before. I know sometimes my husband would give him some money, and he never once told me, "Papa gave me some money." I would give him some money, and my husband would tell me.

INTERVIEWER: **Do you feel that any of that became better or changed?**

AUNT: We talked about it, so I guess it has, because my husband will tell me when he gets some money, but D will never tell me. He'd be telling me he has no money.

CLIENT: If you don't ask me, then…

AUNT: See, now I guess he's not telling nobody, because they're in his business. Yeah. Now I understand that.

INTERVIEWER: **That's a good example. Do you remember a time in particular that was significant as the starting point for resolving your problems? Do you understand the question?**

AUNT: No, not really.

INTERVIEWER: **Do you remember a turning point when you realized a significant starting point or turning point when problems really started to change; when things started looking up?**

AUNT: I remember when he started doing better in school, it started looking up. When he was turning around, I thought, "Hmmm, he's going to make it."

INTERVIEWER: **When you say "turning around," what other things were happening that you noticed?**

AUNT: I noticed he wasn't hanging with the same friends.

CLIENT: I was with the same people. I've been with them since the ninth grade.

AUNT: I didn't see you with these before…with that Mexican boy, and you was talking about getting a nightclub together.

CLIENT: Oh, you mean, owning my own nightclub?

AUNT: Some of them. I can't say all of them were new.

INTERVIEWER: **So any other things that were notable seemed like significant turning points?**

AUNT: He even started doing better in church, didn't he, baby? Started talking in church and stuff.

UNCLE: I don't recall.

AUNT: You don't recall him talking in church? He would get up and do the Sunday school over you and stuff.

UNCLE: I don't know. Did you do that?

CLIENT: Yeah, I would. He would stand in front of a lot of people, talking about…

AUNT: He would start doing it, though.

INTERVIEWER: **But it was something you weren't doing before?**

CLIENT: Yeah.

INTERVIEWER: **Any significant turning points for you, D?**

CLIENT: Nah, I still do what I do.

INTERVIEWER: **Just the clothes, though?**

CLIENT: Yeah, pretty much.

AUNT: Yeah, it was because you and the grandkids came over telling us we ought to be ashamed of ourselves and give his clothes back.

CLIENT: Oh, so other people criticized that.

AUNT: Oh yeah. Big time.

INTERVIEWER: **Any significant turning points for you?**

UNCLE: After we took his clothes, he started doing better, keeping some of his commitments, like doing his chores more.

INTERVIEWER: **Did you know that they noticed these things, D?**

CLIENT: No.

AUNT: Well, I noticed the last time she took his clothes, it was the first time I seen him cry, so I know there was a change, because he was Mr. Tough Man, but that day, he cried.

INTERVIEWER: **Okay, good examples. Next question: Do you remember a moment that you felt like quitting therapy? If so, what made you continue?**

AUNT: I got angry because I saw it did no good for him, and for a while, I wouldn't go. My husband went. Because I was angry. I missed about two. Because I saw it wasn't helping him. He was still hanging with his buddies, because my husband didn't know I went to school a couple of times and saw him at lunchtime, but I never told him. And one time I went looking for him, and they couldn't find him, and I said, "Uh-huh, I ain't even going back. What for?" How about for you, D, a moment you felt like quitting?

CLIENT: I didn't want it, so all the time, I felt like not going.

AUNT: That's why he didn't go.

INTERVIEWER: **What is it about therapy that you didn't want to go?**

CLIENT: It's just somebody else just being in my business. Trying to find out what I'm doing, and it's all taken care of, and I felt like they shouldn't worry about what I'm doing. That's just how I felt about it. She would come here, and that's the only way I would go, because at school, she [the therapist] would send me a pass, and I'd take it, put it in my pocket, and keep doing what I was doing.

INTERVIEWER: **How about you?**

UNCLE: If I get somebody I'm worried about, I'll do it for that one, and there was never a time I didn't want to continue.

INTERVIEWER: **Was it difficult for you to accept the therapist's idea that the problem was not only your son's, but the entire family's problem?**

UNCLE: It wasn't difficult for me, because I knew some things we needed straightening out in terms of our communication. She recognized that and revealed it, and I thought it was good information to help us bring about a better understanding.

INTERVIEWER: **And was it difficult for you to accept that it wasn't only D's problem?**

AUNT: No, it wasn't difficult for me, because I knew it was. It was more than just D's problem.

INTERVIEWER: **Any more you want to add to that?**

AUNT: No, he said it about right.

INTERVIEWER: **Any thoughts from you, D? Did you know or did you feel that that was how the problem was perceived, as a family problem?**

CLIENT: Well, now that I think about it, it was looked at as a family problem, but I didn't feel like…I felt like it was my problem, and I'd get through it and do what I got to do to get through it. I didn't really feel that I needed her help.

INTERVIEWER: **So when you went through the process, you felt more like it was your problem, and you were being made to feel that it was your problem?**

CLIENT: No, that's just how I felt.

INTERVIEWER: **So then you realized, looking back, that it was a family problem?**

CLIENT: No. That how she [the therapist] looked at it, but I felt it was my problem.

INTERVIEWER: **What was your problem?**

CLIENT: The school thing.

INTERVIEWER: **Were you thinking it would have been better to leave out the other half…like have it be just you?**

CLIENT: I felt that it would be better. I guess with her coming in and bringing them into it, I guess that got me confused.

INTERVIEWER: **Okay, very interesting. If you had the same or a different problem again, what would you do?**

UNCLE: Go to Camp A…it's a Christian camp up in northern California. They have a wonderful therapist up there who deals with family problems and issues about how to make family life better.

INTERVIEWER: **Is this something that you found out about after family therapy?**

UNCLE: Yes, I just found out about it two weeks ago. My wife and I were invited up there to work with this group who was making a decision about what the president is going to do with the fifteen billion dollars we have allocated for Africa. That's where we heard about this family therapy done by Al Hollingsworth and his wife, Hattie. The whole idea really is, I would seek out a Christian counselor if we had the same problem.

INTERVIEWER: **Do you think that would have made a difference?**

UNCLE: Sure.

INTERVIEWER: **Can you tell me a little more about what you think would have been different?**

UNCLE: Actually, I have some very good friends who was into Christian counseling, Bishop K, who's a very resourceful person that I usually consult with on matters of importance.

INTERVIEWER: **So was that something you might say was missing from therapy…a Christian element?**

UNCLE: Yes, I think so, because Liliana didn't want to talk about that.

INTERVIEWER: **Oh, okay. She didn't want to talk about that?**

UNCLE: No. Faith and belief were something that was missing in the whole part of our counseling. I think that's a helpful element to…well, actually I believe in the prayer life of the individual. I believe it can help people change their attitudes and aspirations when they pray about it and ask God for direction. I'm a Bible believer. In Proverbs chapter 3 verse 5: "In all thy ways acknowledge him, and he shall rectify."

INTERVIEWER: **Good information. Good input. And for you?**

AUNT: Well, he about said it all. Camp was really nice. I hope we can go back soon.

INTERVIEWER: **So if I understand correctly, if you had the same or different problem again, you would still seek therapy in some form or fashion?**

AUNT: And…

UNCLE: Oh yeah.

INTERVIEWER: **For you, D? If you had the same or different problem again or issues that came up later, what would you do?**

CLIENT: For me, I really didn't like therapy, so therapy wouldn't be my first choice. Say, if I had a problem with someone, I would go to that person, and if we can't resolve it, then...

INTERVIEWER: **What about a personal problem?**

CLIENT: I would talk to somebody who respects me that I can just talk to, and they would just listen 'til I get it all off my chest and feel good.

INTERVIEWER: **That seems to help you?**

CLIENT: Yeah.

INTERVIEWER: **Anything you want to say about this process or anything more that wasn't said in the questions that you could add to the experiences that you had?**

UNCLE: I can't think of anything else.

INTERVIEWER: **Thank you so much for participating, because I know this was a big deal to get together, and I know how it is with time.**

FAMILY #4: HISPANIC FAMILY

Therapist: Dr. Cabouli

Transcription

INTERVIEWER: **If another family came to you and said, "We are going to the program to do what you did," could you explain what it would be like?**

MOTHER: We would say that we started the program with "L," so as to be better parents to our children. We went to the interviews, and "L" set limits and said that each member must occupy a specific place in the home. She also explained how to get along with my husband, to talk often with him. We agreed and disagreed with certain aspects of behavior and abuse within the family. But we wouldn't mention to…

We started going on a weekly basis, and later we started going every other week, every fifteen days. The interviews were very helpful to us, because we didn't know many things, such as how to conduct ourselves with the children, how and when to obey them, how to listen to them, how to care for them. The fact is that—that personally—it was all work, work—with little time devoted to my children. But now, I pay them more attention. What they tell me, put—be in back of them—what's happening, what's not happening, and so forth. This is what family therapy is for.

INTERVIEWER: **And what did your husband think, in spite of the fact that he's not here today? I'd like to hear it from him, but what did he think?**

MOTHER: In the beginning, he argued often with "L."

CLIENT: That it was an obligation to go every week. He didn't like this, because he didn't feel that there was communication between them. In time, he became aware that this would benefit us, not her. She was here to help us, not harm us.

MOTHER: As time passed, he understood the talks we had with "L," and he took a liking to them. He also learned a lot about her. And you, "R"?

CLIENT: It was very good, I enjoyed it. It helped me very much. It changed my way of being.

INTERVIEWER: **What did you think or believe would happen before the therapy?**

MOTHER: There would be talks about what had happened to my daughter—nothing else. We needed help more than anything else. This is why we agreed to go. You must attend all the sessions. We would go because she would teach us to be better parents by giving us "tips" that we could put into practice. And above all, learn.

CLIENT: When I first went to see "L," I thought I was in trouble. Because I said to myself that I had gotten into trouble. But after I got to know her, I realized that she would be a great help to me.

INTERVIEWER: **How did you feel when the entire family went to therapy?**

MOTHER: No, "L" started attending us at our home.

CLIENT: No, at first it was you, myself, and "J" [younger brother], because Dad didn't go. It was at school.

MOTHER: Well, he did this the first time. Then she started coming here to attend all of us. She gathered all of us together. She treated "R" since the children went out, and she treated both of us as a couple. That was her role.

INTERVIEWER: **How did you feel when you were all together?**

MOTHER: We argued with each other: "You do this, you do that, you shouldn't do this." She would guide us, telling us what we should do, what we should say, what we shouldn't say. If the child misbehaved, she told us how to scold him, and that if my husband was the one to scold him, how I should stay out of it, because it would not be correct if I comforted him. If the father scolds, and he comes to me, I should ask him why his father scolded him and make him see that I'm not comforting him but showing him why he mustn't do what he did.

CLIENT: Well, I think I felt ashamed and sad. Everyone stared at me when she walked in. "What's wrong? Why is she here?" Later on, I felt well when she came, because she helped us a lot. I felt I could speak more freely and not hold anything back.

INTERVIEWER: **Can you describe what happened with the therapy, what results each of you obtained?**

MOTHER: It helped me. It helped the entire family. I learned to believe my children, to set limits, to speak with them—they spoke very little. To chat with my husband with whom I had little communication. Whatever he said had to be done. Not anymore, because now I ask him: "Why, because you say so?" I, too, have to give my point of view. Now, my opinion counts.

Now everyone speaks up. "What do you think of this?" "What about that?" Not before—before, when Dad gave an order, it was carried out. This is helping me very much. I would like to continue with the therapy, because one learns something every day. Small incidents appear unexpectedly, and you have to cope with them. She helps you in resolving them.

CLIENT: It helped to talk things out without feeling ashamed. It helped me see what's right and what's wrong. It helped me in getting along with my family, how to express myself. If they trust you, why shouldn't you trust them?

INTERVIEWER: **Tell me about the therapist. What do you think she achieved?**

MOTHER: She made changes around in our family: how we should organize ourselves as a family. She showed me how to share the same household with my daughter, because I have lived with my daughter for a short amount of time. And how to live with my husband—to chat more, to share more with him. We still have a long way to go—have our own private space. But we'll get there, little by little.

She gave us examples, how we need to behave. Because here is another culture—is a different type of life. Here we learn that you need to think about yourself first, yourself second, and yourself third, even if it sounds selfish. First is your own family and yourself. Outside the door, it doesn't matter. That is something we learn from the therapist: that we need to protect the inside, and the outside doesn't matter.

CLIENT: For me, what the therapist did, even if I am repeating myself, she helped me to overcome what was right or wrong—that you had a commitment—that you needed to perform as you committed. She wrote on a paper our agreements, and if we did not follow through, she showed us the paper. She gave us a time frame. She helped us a lot. She taught us that it was not only my father's opinion that counts. I learned that if you want to succeed, you need to think of yourself. She also made us get closer—that my father and mother needed to sleep together, with the baby outside their bed.

INTERVIEWER: **Why did you think that the therapist wanted to see all the family together during the process of therapy?**

MOTHER: Because we all need the therapy. We need to know the opinion of all of us. She did not want to "triangle." She said that—my husband said that. So she wanted all of us to be together.

CLIENT: Because she wanted to help us learn how to live with each other. Not alone, not behind everybody's back—all upfront.

INTERVIEWER: **What was the hardest part of therapy, and what made you continue?**

MOTHER: The harder part was to say what happened and find out more about it. We want to appreciate each other more, my husband and myself—we made the decision that therapy was good for the sake of the family—more for our daughter, but for the good of all of us. That's why we decided not to leave therapy. It was a commitment.

CLIENT: Saying what happened to me—that was the harder part, and also to tell how I was abused. It was very painful to me to talk about that—that's what was the harder part. What made me continue was that I did need help, as all of the family. I continued because I wanted to grow.

INTERVIEWER: **What was the most helpful in the therapy?**

MOTHER: To put limits, because I did not know how to set them, to learn to set boundaries, to listen to my children, to believe them, because they were telling me the truth. With the younger of my children, I learned to do "time out." For my older daughter; to explain why does not need to do a certain thing, why I don't want her to go to a certain place. I learned that [by] talking with the therapist. I try to apply all that I learned.

CLIENT: The therapy taught me more to communicate with my father, and the advice of the therapist helped me. Because if my father gets angry and said something that you know is not as he is saying, I leave him until he calms down, and after that, I say to him that I thought the advice of the therapist was helpful.

INTERVIEWER: **In what ways did the therapist see your problems in a different way than you did?**

MOTHER: She did not see the things different, because she also came from the south. She had experience working with families from M... and A... that are almost the same. Here, the families are different than the Mexican families. She had studied how to work with families in different types of situations and experience than she had. She saw the problems more objectively, because she had studied and we did not study so much. Yes, we had study, but not so much as she did.

CLIENT: Sometimes when you have a problem, even though it is small, you over-exaggerate, you make it bigger, and she did not do that in that way. I think she saw the problems differently because she has more experience, and she knows more about life, because she studied for that.

INTERVIEWER: **How well did your therapist understand you and your problems?**

MOTHER: Because she is a therapist, she studies and sees the case, through her experience, like a medical doctor. Honestly, she understood us, and she has a very good memory. She never forgot what happened in the last session or 15 days before we saw each other. We came and she asked us questions like what happened, what had we done during those 2 weeks that we did not see each other.

CLIENT: She understood me, because she gave me advice—how to improve what I did wrong. I believe the therapist really understood me.

INTERVIEWER: **Did you change the way you viewed your problem at the end of therapy?**

MOTHER: It really changed my point of view of my problems. But the hate for the guy that abused my child; it did not go away. No therapist, even with all the degrees that the therapist has, could take from me this feeling. But right now it is all about supporting my daughter, and that is like a book that I already closed. In reference to other problems, the therapy helped us to change, to give a better solution to our problems.

CLIENT: I believe she did, because at the beginning every thing was dark, very dark. There is a point that you get cold. Today I think twice [about] what I am going to say, I don't answer whatever...I think what I would say, and if it makes sense, I say it.

INTERVIEWER: **Do you remember a time in particular that was significant as the starting point for resolving your problems?**

MOTHER: It was an important confrontation that we had. Neither my husband nor the therapist gave up. I wanted to cry, because my husband was saying that what he was the reality and how things need to be. When the therapist left the session, we said that you find the size of your shoes. Things really changed since that point.

I learned that, as a woman, you need to appreciate yourself. You don't need to give up on what you really think. I was the type of woman that, if my husband said green, I said green, even if he was wrong. Right now is different. And it was at that time, the therapist used to ask me what I was feeling, what was going on with me—that I don't need to be silent, that I need to have an opinion, that my voice also counts.

INTERVIEWER: **Do you remember a moment that you felt like quitting therapy? If so, what made you continue?**

MOTHER: No, we felt bad when the therapist said that she thought everything was good, and that we don't need therapy anymore. My younger son did not want to go to therapy—he wanted to go to another place. My husband, at the beginning, saw that as an obligation. At the beginning, he did not want to go. After a while, he began to see the positive side to the treatment. He saw that it was good for us. It was really important to us, the meetings with the therapist. We attended all the sessions—only one that she changed the place where we met, and we couldn't find the place.

INTERVIEWER: **Was it difficult for you to accept the fact that the problem was not your daughter or son's problem, but the entire family's problem?**

MOTHER: Honestly, the problem was not only my daughter's problem. It was the whole family's problem. I always felt like that, and I continue thinking in that way. She was not guilty about what happened to her. The problem was that we did not take care as we should; we realized in the therapy. The therapist pushed a lot of our issues and confronted us—what the family needed to resolve, how we can overcome obstacles.

CLIENT: I thought I was guilty—guilty for the abuse—and I realized that I wasn't, and I felt relieved.

INTERVIEWER: **If you had the same or a different problem again, what would you do?**

MOTHER: I would talk about it, I would talk about the problem we have. We all give opinions, and we come to the conclusion, and you resolve it. Problems in the school, I talk with the principal in the school.

CLIENT: I talk to my parents, and I look for help with them.

MOTHER: It was very good, the program I would like to continue growing as a family. My daughter is all changed. She has not had any problems in school. She made a drastic change—a very good one.

SECOND INTERVIEW: CAUCASIAN, MASTER-LEVEL THERAPIST

SUPERVISED BY DR. CABOULI

INTERVIEWER: **If another family came to you and said, "We are going to go to the program to do what you did"; could you explain what it would be like?**

RATIMA: (Client had therapy before, since she was five years old. She found a major difference) Therapy with Anna, in general, was very helpful: she was there for the relationship. She is really good at what she does. Anna is the first person ever to show concern for my problems and feelings. She doesn't just sit there with a pen and paper and expect money. Every other therapist had sessions of fifteen to twenty minutes, even though they are supposed to have an hour session. They are just sitting there, and taking notes and giving no feedback. Then you go home nothing to work on, with no types of skills to move forward, and it is basically me there venting out about what is going on with me. They just reschedule and say, "see you in two weeks." And then I met Anna, which was a completely different experience. She has been wonderful, absolutely wonderful. I don't want to lose her.

EDUARDO: You won't believe this, but the first time I met Anna, I told her that I don't trust her. But she explained to me that trust is a growing process. Just the fact that she was Caucasian; I think they come from bad culture. I approached her that way, meanwhile, she was coming to counsel me and my dysfunctional family. I developed trust because Anna is down to earth. She is not traditional.

INTERVIEWER: **What did you expect would happen in the program before you went there?**

EDUARDO: I was distrustful.

RATIMA: Me, I was very nervous. I was expecting somebody who would place judgment on my family, on my living conditions; and I expected what I usually got. Somebody there is waiting for the time to go by and the next patient to arrive.

EDUARDO: For me, the time just flew by

INTERVIEWER: **What was it like for you to bring your whole family to therapy?**

RATIMA: I was nervous, and it was scary. There were a lot of issues involved. At the beginning, it was embarrassing, but Anna took that embarrassment away and was understanding.

EDUARDO: It is a unique experience, I have never had anything other sort. [Client had never had therapy).

INTERVIEWER: **Can you describe what happened in therapy? What was it like for each of you?**

RATIMA: Anna made me realize the issues that I am hurting from. She made me realize that there is hope for my family, and there is hope for me. Just because I have problems right now, it does not make me a bad person.

EDUARDO: Anna has helped me to rekindle some feelings with my wife. It is a reward for me. Anna gave me an opportunity to sit down, first once a week, then once a month, to talk about some serious stuff, where my wife and I can't exactly do it.

INTERVIEWER: **Tell me about your therapist and what she did?**

RATIMA: She did not place judgment on us. She was down to earth and treated us as real people. I feel very comfortable with her, and I feel like I can be open and honest with anything, no matter what issue it is.

INTERVIEWER: **Why do you think that your therapist wanted to see all the members of the family participating in the process?**

RATIMA: Because it is a family issue, and Anna has specifically stated that, unless we are all willing to participate and all are willing to give a a hundred percent, she will never be able to help us, and I agree with her. Otherwise it is a waste of her time.

EDUARDO: On several occasions, Anna made it clear that she is an advocate for the family. She could help Rebecca with her decision to move on, but she is really here to try to get this family functioning.

INTERVIEWER: **What was the most difficult part of therapy, and what made you continue?**

RATIMA: The most difficult part for me was facing my drug abuse; to tell Anna that I used. I felt ashamed of myself, I felt embarrassed. I am a mom, and it is not the right behavior for a mom. But Anna did not make me feel like a bad person. She was understanding and let me know that I can get better. It has subsided since I met Anna. It made me continue, because she did not place judgment on me, and she let me know that we can work through this; and the fact that she is an advocate for the family.

EDUARDO: Opening up. I continued because of her declaration about being an advocate to my family. I recognized that my family needs counseling. I think now that people need to sit down once in a while and talk about what they really feel.

RATIMA: He was not for this Anna thing. He was so against it and so against bringing people into our home. He felt that they will place judgment on us, take our kids away. Anna really showed us that she is not there to place judgment, she is not there to pick up the phone and call the police. She knows that we are good people trying to create a family, and we just need some more tools how to fix the problems. Every family has problems, and not everybody knows how to deal w those problems. She gave us some tools to deal with those problems, and it is wonderful.

INTERVIEWER: **What do you think was helpful in therapy? Describe it and explain why.**

The therapist not being judgmental and was accepting, and she expressed advocacy to the entire family.

INTERVIEWER: **In what ways did the therapist see your problems in a different way than you did?**

RATIMA: She realized that I recognize that I have problems, but yet, I haven't made the proper steps to fix those problems. Like she said, I do a lot of talking without acting, and today she made me realize you can't just talk about it, but must do it. She saw it in a different light than I did.

EDWIN: She simply saw things in an outside view, not someone who is emotionally attached.

INTERVIEWER: **How well did your therapist understand you and your problems?**

RATIMA: One hundred percent. She understood, totally. She is very down to earth, very non-judgmental and she realized that we have a lot to work on. It is going to take some baby-steps to get where we need to be. She didn't ever put in an expectation that it is a job for a twenty-four-hour period.

EDUARDO: In some cases, it was too clear that she did understand. It was only during the later visits that she come to recognize what she was really dealing with. It was like a stepping stone on understanding. But she did understand a good deal.

INTERVIEWER: **Did you change the way you viewed your problem at the end of therapy?**

EDUARDO: Yes. I recognize now that I have been destroying my wife's self esteem with my harsh words. It is really difficult. I may be sometimes too real. I have no way to explain people without being offensive. I could refrain from profanity easy, but sometime the words come out.

REBECCA: Yes. I don't use drugs as often, and before I started to see Anna, I was really embarrassed about having family issues, now not anymore. She made feel like it is okay, it is normal.

INTERVIEWER: **Do you remember a time in particular that was significant as the starting point for resolving your problems?**

RATIMA: When she has these sessions in her office. She had these sessions where, instead of venting and going back and forth: "You, you, you, I, I, I," she did constructive things. She put the radio on and had us standing, holding hands the whole time. We had to look each other in the eye, and there was no time where he had to face away from each other, and she would ask a question, or she would say a statement, and we would have to complete the statement with our own response. Those things helped us understand that we weren't there for a venting session; she actually had tools to help on working the problems we have.

EDUARDO: I think like Rebecca said; we have said nice things to one another. I think we made love that night.

INTERVIEWER: **Do you remember a moment that you felt like quitting therapy? If so, what made you continue?**

RATIMA: No.

EDUARDO: No.

INTERVIEWER: **Was it difficult for you to accept the fact that the problem was not your son/daughter's problem, but the entire family's problem?**

RATIMA: Not for me.

EDUARDO: Sure, it was a little difficult.

INTERVIEWER: **If you had the same or a different problem again, what would you do?**

RATIMA; I would call Anna.

EDUARDO: I would seek counseling; the one thing I never thought I would. I thought counseling was for dysfunctioning people; I never thought I was dysfunctioning. I am not perfect.

ANOTHER INTERVIEW:

EUROPEAN , MASTER-LEVEL THERAPIST
therapist supervised by Dr.Cabouli

INTERVIEWER: **If another family came to you and said, "We are going to go to the program to do what you did"; could you explain what it would be like?**

VALERIA: I think that she made me open my eyes; made me more realistic about life, and that is why I recommend anybody to go to therapy. It started with the whole experience inside; making you understand the logic of what is going on; making you understand in a better way. Basically, it makes you stronger. That is part of life, but sometimes, people don't understand that. Those problems come from regular life. Everybody has problems. Some people take it different ways: some get depressed, some people take it in anger, some become sad and let themselves fall. But in my case, it made me stronger for my kids.

She is pretty good. Besides being realistic, she is scary. I met her in a very, on the street, in public. She heard my problems, and she did not even care about my insurance; she went in and she solved the problem first. I was going through a very big crisis, and she took me out of it. And she took the whole "being involved," and she was right there for me. I will never forget that. You don't find many people like that. Lots of people are greedy. I had two different therapists before, and they were all about the billing and the insurance, without caring for me. In fact, I had a lot of problems with that, because they released personal information to people that they shouldn't. They should have asked me to sign something. She is very legal and loyal. She does the right thing; you know how it is in the system. She went in the right way. She has, you know, integrity.

INTERVIEWER: **What did you expect would happen in the program before you went there?**

VALERIA: Get out and get better.

INTERVIEWER: **What was it like for you to bring your whole family to therapy?**

VALERIA: Yes, I brought my family, but not my ex-husband.

INTERVIEWER: **Can you describe what happened in therapy? What was it like for each of you?**

VALERIA: She was trying to find out; first of all, she fixed the crisis. I was going through a big crisis. She was giving me therapy, and later on, when the crisis went away, we started going into deep stuff; you about what was the problem, try to find me. Who Sandra was, beside my kids because I always care about my kids and I put my kids front of my needs. And she made me understand that it is just as important to make yourself happy before somebody else. Exterior stuff first, than more personal. We went through a lot of concentration and reading exercising--- self work.

INTERVIEWER: **Tell me about your therapist and what she did?**

VALERIA: Within the answer to the first question

INTERVIEWER: **Why do you think that your therapist wanted to see all the members of the family participating in the process?**

VALERIA: Because she thought that part of my whole problem was my whole family. We went through domestic violence. Every single one of us needed therapy, so we did individual therapy and family therapy. Even my kid, who lives in San Francisco, but was not part of domestic violence; is a very important person of my family. The kids look up at him, because he is the oldest. I have four children.

INTERVIEWER: **What was the most difficult part of therapy, and what made you continue?**

VALERIA: The most difficult part was being able to tell the whole truth to somebody you don't know. It is about very personal things. In a way, she made me balanced, so I can open up that way. It is over; I put that stuff in another place in my life. Like I said before, when I see my kids' faces and how they keep going and fighting it, and they keep getting better; it is like an inspiration to me.

INTERVIEWER: **What do you think was helpful in therapy? Describe it and explain why.**

VALERIA: Therapy with the whole family and the way she worked it out; individual and then together, and bringing everybody to talk about every problem in the family, and then fixing it on the individual; doing the breathing and the concentration. I started to do meditation, and that helps a lot.

INTERVIEWER: **In what ways did the therapist see your problems in a different way than you did?**

VALERIA: It was that she made me understand that it was my own fault in a way, because I made bad decisions. Basically, it was the result of my bad decisions. I should have taken over and looked better and gotten to know people better; one after and other. And I keep choosing the same stereotyped guy. She made me understand that everything has consequences, you know, and so if I make bad choices, I am going to have bad luck. The best thing to do is to try to get to know people more and not to be that close to trusting someone until I get to know them.

INTERVIEWER: **How well did your therapist understand you and your problems?**

VALERIA: Very good. In the beginning, she was little bit frustrated, because she couldn't believe that I made those decisions and stuff, but she put herself in my shoes and said, "You know, I feel bad for you for everything you went through, and I understand." She was very understanding. Also, she made me become responsible. I was always very responsible, but punctuality was very important. You know, with so many kids and so many tasks with one person, it is kind of hard to be punctual; but I try my best, and now I try to schedule my things ahead of time. She taught me that. She basically brings me back. I used to be that way, but then, with all those things going on, she brought me back.

INTERVIEWER: **Did you change the way you viewed your problem at the end of therapy?**

VALERIA: Yes.

INTERVIEWER: **Do you remember a time in particular that was significant as the starting point for resolving your problems?**

VALERIA: In the middle, when doing the whole family work. It was, like, step by step.

INTERVIEWER: **Do you remember a moment that you felt like quitting therapy? If so, what made you continue?**

VALERIA: Yeah, I moved far away from her. I was driving, the baby and driving to work, and not sleeping enough, because I have a nighttime job. She was like, a little bit pushy with me, and she made me understand: "Listen, one day you have to fix this, and if you don't fix this, you are not going to get better." I realized from the beginning that she was good, because of the way she started and the way she cared. She made me understand that it was really helping me; it was really waking me up. I saw the difference, so it made me say that I want to get better.

INTERVIEWER: **Was it difficult for you to accept the fact that the problem was not your son/ daughter's problem, but the entire family's problem?**

VALERIA: Yes, I did. Once it effects you, the head of the family; basically, you do everything for them. If they have a problem, it affects me, so I think it is the whole family. One has a problem, and the whole family has a problem.

INTERVIEWER: **If you had the same or a different problem again, what would you do?**

VALERIA: I would not let that happen. She made me understand. I got that worked out. For me, being here and talking about it like nothing, is major for me. I recommend people to her. If you would ever be in a problem like this, I would run again to get counseling. Keeps you awake, reminds you what is good what is bad. I would get more directive therapy. It sounds kind of cruel at the beginning, but I think it works. When you are being realistic, you say wake up, this is what it is like. If you don't get it that way, you won't get it at all. Some people need to be soft, but it does not work.

TEACHING STRATEGIC EXPERIENTIAL FAMILY THERAPY.

The most scary and exciting thing that has happened to me was when I taught this model for the first time at AIU.

I had nine students, all anxious and not knowing what to expect. I felt the same way as they did, but I was willing to risk giving a hundred percent of my best, hoping that the experience would be a growing one.

I created an outline that would teach people my model by experiencing what the model is about, and also by pushing them out of their comfort zone. During the process, they expressed different emotions and levels of awareness, but one thing I am sure of - we all grew from our experience together. Below are some things they had to say about the class and the model .

It is important to understand that as a therapist, you will not take your clients where you have never been and where you are not willing to go. For me, training people in this model is promoting the learning of the exercises through their own experiences.

If I see a student that cannot take feedback from their classmates, I know that student will not be good at promoting that in a family system. If someone cannot confront or take confrontation, they will not be able to do it with a family or a relationship.

Being in my classroom is different than practicing therapy, because it involves explanations, lectures and a willingness to participate.

Strategic Experiential therapists are driven people with an internal desire to grow, people who strive for high self esteem and are willing to stand up in the middle of a room and disagree if they really do. They are real and caring professionals.

I enjoy being a professor and sometimes agonize over it at the same time. When my students open up and trust the process of learning in this way, it makes it worth the effort. When people open up to who they really are, with no defenses and with no resistance, we can experience the beauty of being human and the greatness of intimacy and real connection. I wish to promote this in the universe as my contribution towards a more loving, caring world. This is my calling.

STUDENT #1

Cabouli developed in me the confidence I needed move from "student" therapist to therapist. She taught that you need to be yourself first and bring the best of yourself into the therapeutic relationship; the treatment plans and techniques will come later. She challenges you in a way that helps you to define yourself as a therapist. I don't know what my side-talking or tug-of-war resisting is all about, but I could just lump all of that into the category of immaturity and genuine resistance to change.

Student #2

The Wisdom is Mounting

As a well-known Gestalt therapist, Walter Kemper said that wisdom comes from personal experience, not from personal knowledge. I do learn some wisdom of psychotherapy from my experience in this class. Let me share some experience and my awareness via being in this class.

Partly because I am a foreign student and English is my second language, I strongly need some structure in the class in order to protect myself in front of any class in the United States. Thus, when I found this class was not as structural as other classes were, I knew some challenges were coming. Due to the safe atmosphere which Dr. Cabouli made lots of efforts to create, I felt comfortable with being myself and disclosing my real issues, instead of playing an "Americanized" role, which I play very often in the United States. I still think this class is unique and necessary for most therapist trainees. I believe that being a therapist not only results from reading textbooks and case studies, or doing therapy, but also from exploring themselves in some special moments or therapy experience.

Unleash my Armed

When I read the letters in front of the class, I could hear my inner voice of sadness and isolation, I could feel that the voice wanted to be heard, healed, and consulted. I followed my body message to let it go. I appreciated the nonverbal security we created in the class. The invisible atmosphere got me into the group and unleashed my "armed." I totally felt safe and pleasant in that class. At that moment, I really think the verbal barrier cannot inhibit the connection among human psyches. Meanwhile, I would like to mention a movement Dr. Cabouli made for me at that night. She came to me and hugged me. This was the most powerful, therapeutic experience that I ever experienced. At that specific moment, I felt that I could rely on someone and completely unleash my armed role in order to integrate any part of myself. Because of my culture, I am not used to hugging people; yet I could not find that any intervention would produce a better therapeutic effectiveness to me than that simple hug.

Take a Risk

In the fourth week, we did an intimate exercise with our partners. Honestly, I did not feel comfortable in the beginning of the exercise. Looking at a new friend at such a close distance makes me anxious. No only is she female, but also conflicts my past patterns. Face to face in a one-foot distance is more difficult to me than hugging a partner. At such a close distance, I can feel certain upward intimacy between us, but at the same time, I also feel awkward, because it is not a regular interaction that I would like to make with someone I just met. However, once the interaction ended, I could find certain level of trust between myself and my partner. What an amazing tactic! I think this intimate interaction could be one of the best exercises for most couples who need to boost their intimacy. Due to my rigid and more traditional background, I may have difficulties in embracing people who tend to show their enthusiasm directly and physically. I know it is time to break up my old frame in order to get close people from diverse cultures. I am going to take a risk expanding my personal boundaries. Good luck to myself!

Clients Dislike Therapists

I strongly agree with the concept that therapists' jobs are not to make clients love them, but to make clients change; and further, don't be afraid of clients' dislike. It is hard to keep in mind, even though I hear this line several times. Sometimes the therapists' personalities are apt to please people. I am one of these types of people and I do not feel comfortable with provoking clients' emotions. I have to admit that this is my issue in therapy. Fortunately, I am more aware of my traits, and I started changing the pattern of my therapy. In that therapy session, I was provoked by Dr. Cabouli's criticism, instead of agreeing with her condemnation. Thus, I could feel that I wanted to try something to prove her opinion was wrong. I can imagine that this paradoxical strategy will produce huge impacts on certain people. In summary, there are a myriad of ways to change clients. Therapists should have more options of intervening in the dynamics of families, rather than holding one fixed strategy.

STUDENT #3

My experience with this model has been good thus far. This model makes a lot of sense to me, as someone who is still fine-tuning a name to what is done in therapy, overall. I naturally come at therapy from a more cognitive approach, but as time has gone on, there has been a bigger component of experiential. In therapy, getting at the emotions in the room as the client is talking about the symptom is helpful, so that they connect with the moment and start to see the effects on them and everyone around them. In therapy, honesty is important, and the relationship is the first and most important thing to develop and strengthen. The struggle that occurs for me is being more connected with the clients' emotions. I see it in session and can point it out, but there is a part of me that does not always feel it. The challenge for me is to be able to soften myself so that I am there in the moment with the client, rather than just being able to ask questions, for the client to start talking about the feeling. The therapist needs to feel it, too.

The first stage of the approach, the motivational stage, is necessary for me in therapy. Some theories do not put much emphasis on joining with the client, and many do not have it as a distinct stage. Having the therapist put specific emphasis on developing a relationship with the client right from the beginning allows for a more intimate trust to be developed, more risk-taking to be done, and potentially, more change occurring for the good. This stage also appears to be the assessment stage, where the therapist is joining, but also figuring out the family dance and what dynamics are present. Understanding where the family is coming from culturally is important, also, and this is the place where it starts.

In the discussion of the second stage of therapy, reframing the problem as a family problem, examples are given where the family is told how they all have a place in the dance, and how marital conflict effects the family as a whole. In American society, I do not believe that couples really understand how much impact their communication, both verbal and nonverbal, has on their children, specifically communication in the marriage. Reframing the problem as a family problem is important. It can be difficult when the whole family is not present or is not willing to hear the therapist take the blame away from the IP and put it into a more neutral zone. This stage is where I see more strategic components come into play. I am not as connected in the strategic piece as I am to the experiential. However, I am learning the usefulness of a more strategic approach, and find that I use more strategy than I realized before taking this class.

I like the third stage, where de-balancing and setting boundaries occurs. I work with children and families a lot and am teaching parenting and communication skills. Being able to role-model boundaries and teach different ways to perceive hierarchy in the family can be very important. Making sure that the parents are not pulling any of the children into the marital subsystem or lowering down to the child's subsystem is challenging, but a very important part of therapy. In this, I see strategy and being very direct coming into play.

Stage four is emotional, and an area I have a hard time with; not because I don't see the client is hurting or where fears lie. I have trouble with how to be with the client fully. I tend to get involved only partway. However, I am taking this class as a way to develop this more, and I can say that my classes with EFT and SEFT have given me a new view on how to be able to connect emotionally to the emotion that clients are experiencing. Being real and focusing on the present and the process are key to me.

I like the idea of identifying the cycles that families have, and with this identification of the cycles in stage four, the change can happen and begin sticking. Insight into the cycles can help to motivate and change the cycle. I see stage five as appropriately labeled as "the power-struggle stage," as there is bound to be a great deal of resistance to change.

The last stage is difficult for me to understand. I see that it is work with the parents and differentiation; however, I am not sure how it fits in as the end stage with the rest of the therapy. I think that there is a component where the parents are encouraged to use what they have learned with their family of origin. I may see this fitting into the beginning of therapy more or throughout, rather than at the end. Regardless of where it is in the stages of this theory, the parents working on family-of-origin issues can be a very powerful and influential piece in the change process for the family that originally came for family therapy. A common saying fits well here: "We learn what we live, and then we live what we learn."

STUDENT #4

I think that the model introduced in class is a very interesting blend of important aspects of various prominent systemic family theories represented in its six stages: motivation (joining and blending); reframing the problem as a family problem; rebalancing and setting boundaries; the emotional stage of intergenerational connections; the power struggle stage; and the insight oriented-stage.

I agree that the first, most important, step of successful therapy is joining with the clients. I believe that clients will not be able to open up and provide information if they do not feel comfortable and do not trust the process that takes place in therapy. This fact was made evident during some of the exercises that took place in class. For example, I noticed that the first time I participated in the relaxation exercise, I was not as calm and relaxed as I was when the same exercise was repeated later on. I really believe that this has to do with the fact of unfamiliarity and not knowing exactly what to expect from this class and people around me at the very beginning. I also agree with the importance that the model places on the development of the cultural sensitivity on the part of the therapist. For example, all of us in this class come from different backgrounds and were raised in various cultures and families; each of them with their own unique set of values and cultural norms. I have observed how some of us are more expressive and outgoing, and others more reserved and quieter. Some of us have opened up right away, and others have taken a while to be able to share.

However, I think, it is also important not to assume that, just because somebody appears outgoing and/or comes from a culture where people are usually very expressive, that this person will be expressive and open from the very beginning. Taking into consideration personal characteristics of the individual as well as the specific life circumstances he/she is in, is also a very important aspect to take into consideration.

The last observation regarding this stage is the attempt that the therapist in this model makes to create alliances with different family members. I have observed that the same attempts have been made in class through various exercises we all have participated in, such as the circle we make at times and the holding hands, the greeting, and the hugging that took place in a couple of occasions, or the guided imagery; just to mention a few. These experiential exercises definitely had a powerful impact on me, and I would assume for other students in class, as well.

The third stage of the model that has to do with de-balancing and setting boundaries is also very important.

Again, just observing the family-of-origin exercises in class, I noticed the importance of establishing such boundaries. This experience, and others with my own family of origin, as well the experience of working with other families, has taught me that families, just like any other institutions, have their own hierarchies, such as the parental subsystem and other subsystems subordinate of the parental subsystem, such as the sibling subsystem. If this hierarchy is reversed with children assuming parental roles, the family will be thrown into serious chaos. I do agree with the model that it is very important to teach parenting skills and communication skills to family members. Also, I agree with the important caution, made during this stage, of the expected resistance and active role the therapist needs to take to bring this resistance; of course, assuming that he/she has already gained the family's trust. At the same time, these exercises have reinforced my belief that cultural sensitivity is very important regarding the degree of challenging the resistance in the family and/or among certain family members.

I do believe that learning to communicate openly without becoming defensive is very important. It allows the family members to be able to resolve conflict in a constructive manner, which also leads to increasing individual family members' level of self-esteem. I agree that this stage can be very difficult and scary. I agree that teaching families how to alter their perhaps, long-rooted, dysfunctional ways of communication can be quite a challenging job, but I also believe it is possible. For example, there has been quite a resistance in class on the part of various students while attempting to accomplish various tasks, especially when it comes to communicating their thoughts and feelings. However, I think it has been possible on the part of a number of students to open up, whereas there are still others who continue to struggle Therefore, I agree with the emphasis the model places on first working with family-of-origin issues before trying to achieve communication and increased self-esteem. It makes sense, for example, that if a person has experienced rejection and/or abuse, he/she will not be able to open up and express his/her feelings. I think it is a very interesting point, as mentioned in the model, that family members need to "emotionally understand what patterns they are repeating, and experience the pain that is hidden and projected into the IP." It is true; it is the pain that is caused from previous generation(s) that people sometimes bring down to their nuclear families, causing to their own family members the same pain that was previously caused to them by others in their family of origin. Furthermore, experiential exercises mentioned in the model, such as imaginary guidance and writing letters to parents, can be very powerful techniques, as we all experienced and observed in class. Also, role-playing (which we have also utilized in class) and the empty-chair technique are other powerful techniques, the latter especially important when the family member(s) is (are) not available.

I do believe that the power-struggle stage is another important one that needs to be recognized. I agree that families have the tendency to resist change, wanting to return to past, unproductive behaviors. I do believe that the therapist at this stage while continuing to be caring, needs to also be assertive reminding everybody in the family of their achievements and also of the consequences if they go back to their old ways of communicating and behaving.

The insight-oriented stage is also very important, as it deals with the parental subsystem or, in some cases, the most differentiated parent. I agree with the model that a lot of education takes place during this stage through teaching the parents about triangles and alliances. The cultural aspect is a very important one to be taken into consideration, given that differentiation does not even exist in the lexicon of some cultures, such as Albanian; therefore, trying to teach such parents concepts that are foreign to them can be damaging and can even lead to the risk of alienation.

Finally, another important point made in this model is that the stages can overlap. I agree that there is not a formula that says when the therapist "should" become more active or passive, more caring or distant. I think that it is important that the therapist follows the family's lead and does not bring his/her own agenda into the session. I would say that the magic word here would be "flexibility," side by side with the sensitivity, caring and expertise we bring as therapists in the counseling session!

STUDENT #5

Okay, well, I am going to start off by saying thank you so much for your honesty as a practicum teacher. I am going to be honest, though, after leaving your class, I am struggling finding a theory that works for me. I thought I was more of a narrative therapist, until I experienced your class, and now that I know your theory is extremely successful, I am struggling trying to incorporate this into my practice. I have discussed this with many people, and I have come to the conclusion that I am simply not comfortable with my skills in the room, yet, in order to read the clients the way that you do. I guess I am somewhat fearful of making a huge mistake. I am hoping and assuming that I will acquire this skill with time, and that someday, I will be the next American Liliana with a radio show and all. I honestly value your work so much and thank you for being true to yourself and us as your students. Although your style may not have suited everyone in the class, I know you had an extremely positive impact on most of us. I speak very highly of you and have referred numerous students to you who I thought would work well with you and your form of therapy. I wish I could be as honest as you.

STUDENT #6

Something I want to tell you:

Thank you.

First of all, I would like to thank you for your efforts. I sincerely appreciated your enthusiasm and passion during the whole summer. For example, in the rebirth activity, you did whatever you could do physically to make sure you safely held onto each one. I saw you sweating, and you almost ran out of energy, but I also could feel your determination in providing everyone a safe and trusting environment. I was moved by your action during the rebirth activity. Meanwhile, your passion pushed me to challenge myself to do something different, and your enthusiasm reinforced my dream of how lucky I am for being a therapist! Knowing what you have done in this field expands my plan for my future. As you said in the class, we should not be limited by a tradition role of therapist. We could create different services for different ethnic groups. For me, I started thinking about how to market myself as a therapist in my own culture, even in the whole Chinese society. I started dreaming that I could do something different to contribute to my country. Also, I could create different ways to approach those people who are not familiar with psychotherapy. It is true that therapists cannot just sit in their offices to wait for their clients to come. Instead, therapists can do something creative and meaningful to expand their services. I like this idea, and I really started thinking about it. Finally, the safe moment you and each one created in class gave me more of a sense of security to explore myself in an exotic environment. To be honest, I doubted what we could do in the beginning of this class, even though I had lots of experience with joining group therapy in the past. Later on, I was moved by your unquestionable determination and your caring and trustful mind. Since then, I knew I could take a risk in this class, because I knew you would protect us, even though you challenged our actions. Sincerely, I thank you for your effort to make this class successful and worthwhile. Thank you.

What I have learned:

I want you to know that I really learned some things from this class. First, I started again working on my family of origin, instead of merely talking about my family issue on the paper. That was a huge difference between this class and other classes. It is no doubt that, because of this class, I started some actions instead of thinking my issues as usually. Action is based on my thinking, but executing action is much harder than getting some insights. Due to this class, especially to your pushing, I stepped out of my safe circle to take a risk in my personal journey. This motivation resulted from the atmosphere of this class. The atmosphere in this class not only provided me safety, but also challenged my old safe patterns. It sounds paradoxical that the atmosphere could be both safe and unsafe. This experience is like learning how to swim. People feel safe because of a coach around them, but they also feel anxious because they cannot swim. In that situation, a great coach will push those beginners to explore their abilities, instead of letting them stay in a safe place. Certainly, the only way to be able to swim is to take the risk of swimming alone. I started swimming away from my "coach" or my old "safe" territory.

In addition, I have a different sense about what experiential strategy family therapy is. By reading your book in the beginning of this summer, I thought I knew what ESFT was. Yet it was extremely different when I experienced this approach during this class. By involving myself into this specific approach in this class, I gained some wisdom which already existed in my mind, beyond the superficial knowledge. I am sure that this wisdom will become a therapeutic aid, and I am also confident about how to use this wisdom in my practice. However, I know it would have been different if this class had not been employed in this experiential way. I wonder whether or not I could learn this wisdom if this class was a lecture class rather than an experiential class.

Difficulties in this class:

Even though I got such wonderful experience from this class, and I strongly recommend that everyone should take this class, it will be difficult to spread this class among MFT students in the future. Definitely, I could expect that some students in the future may resist those amazing experiences. At that point, I it would be hard to grade them and it would feel difficult dealing with those students if I were a professor in this class. Thus, it is important to define what the class means and how to grade. It could perhaps help to differentiate the process of the class from the content of the class;

because each one has a different level of disclosure and a different agreement to taking a risk, it is hard to expect everyone to push themselves with their level of efforts. Accordingly, it is hard to differentiate or grade students' performance. As a member of this class, I knew it was hard for Kerreen to explore herself at this moment. I did understand what she felt in this class, because I experienced that process before. I was not affected by her non-involvement, but I did wonder what the experience would be if half of the students in the future decided not to involve themselves. From the bottom of my heart, I recommend that every therapist-trainee take this class, but I can also imagine how hard it will be to lead various students in a room to get some experiential wisdoms. Sincerely, Dr. Cabouli, you did a extremely wonderful job!

STUDENT #7

What I Want You To Know Is...

We like to laugh and have fun with the adventure of being ourselves. We are comfortable in our own skin. We pride ourselves in our ability to genuine. We are warm. We love people. I respect your passion. Even more, I respect your ability to be so successful in a new culture. It takes tremendous courage and chutzpah to do what you have done in a new country. I love the way you truly want to share your wisdom with us, your students. I respect your courage to be vulnerable.

I look to connect, to stimulate, to challenge, to appreciate, and to be a "self." The self of the therapist develops over many years. Indeed, you have had a decisive part in my identity development as a therapist. Celebrate the ripples of influence you make on me and in other future doctors of psychology! Applaud us for our fervent attempts to get clearer about what WE think, especially as you attempt to convey the sense and spirit of your own thinking about families.

I want you to know that you have been an inspiration in reminding me of the way our profession has empowered us to do this. You are the embodiment of the idea that dreams can, and do, come true. Thank you from my heart for sharing of yourself, for inspiring us to push forward in our personal journeys, and for encouraging us to be therapists who make a difference!

STUDENT #8

What I Want You To Know 2

I remember I was totally drained after ten minutes of being around you the first few times I was around you, and I still don't know what that's all about. Perhaps I just knew that you would probably say something direct and upfront that would push my buttons and my resistance, which just wore me out until I had to stop resisting and realize that, whatever you said might shock me, make me angry, or piss me off, or whatever;

that you have sincere and positive intentions and would only say things that you felt had some purpose in my improvement. I know I will grow to be an excellent therapist with you as my mentor, if you would mentor me. I would love to be able to learn your model and get lots of experience. I know that I could learn your model and still be able to do your model while making it fit my personality, because it is not about being a cookie-cutter therapist following a specific number of steps the same way each and every time.

I am also so surprised and shocked that, in the two months that I have known you, you have helped me be more of an honest and authentic person. Even though it is hard and painful for me to go

STUDENT #9

Imaginary Guidance:

My experience of imaginary guidance was somewhat distracting this time.

Going back to my childhood home and meeting myself and parents was a very strong tool for working and experiencing unfinished business.

In my case, I was not aware of what was my unfinished business, so I could not relate what to experience in my mind when I was doing imaginary guidance, but reminded me of all the fun things I did with my parents.

It could be because my house was a place to laugh and receive comfort and security most of the time.

I think the awareness came through when members and you challenged my assumption of coming from healthy family.

I started questioning myself and how my parents had treated me.

I always had a hard time defining what is "normal" and "not normal".

I always thought gaining insight would make me grow and be set free, but I then realized it was not all about insight, but it was real awareness that is the beginning of growth.

I still have hard time understanding what happened that made me aware...

But I'd learned a very important thing; that is everyone needs to get in touch with real emotions within themselves and create connection with important ones. Otherwise, it will not bring true change.

Family of Origin:

When I studied about family of origin at school, it was focused more on observable recursive pattern in family (alcoholic, cut-off, fused), never really learned to see emotional pattern in family.

Not seeing something obvious but seeing something underlying their behaviors and how it has been a pattern in generations was very fascinating but at the same time, I felt that I need more experiences and practice.

For example, I knew that "not identifying emotions was" a pattern in my mom's family but I didn't know the "way they do not identify" was by manipulation and rationalization. I also didn't know it was all done to protect family members (especially fragile member in family), this, in depth emotional family of origin that I experience is truly insightful.

I loved the exercise and makes me practice this exercises to get better sense of work.

STUDENT #10

Letter to Dr. C

I want to thank you yet again. This time I knew I would be on a roller coaster. But this time I knew that you had inspected the roller coaster for safety before I got on. I was able to trust so much more in this training because everyone wanted to grow so much. I thank you for supportively pushing me as always and for instinctively knowing when I had enough and needed some support (or a hug!!). I cannot tell you how much insight and awareness I gained from this training. I described the training as lightning speed therapy. I felt like I had been jolted alive each week and stirred in some way that would be helpful to me. At times, I just felt like I could not handle it, but I was able to see that I can. I feel so much stronger as a person and as a therapist. I feel like that groundwork has been laid out for me to permanently continue this personal growth process. I find myself sometimes feeling as though I have learned so much that there cannot be that much more. Your class showed me that there is always much more awareness to be gained. I have seen the transmission of family dynamics of my family and feel empowered to handle the impact of these dynamics. At the same time, this training provoked my anxiety and reduced it by stirring things up, identifying them, and then problem solving. It has been such a pleasure to get to know people on such an intimate level as this is so the opposite of my real life. I have also enjoyed getting to know myself so much more and my willingness to be vulnerable and take risks. I cannot even go through all that I have learned as it would be a book. I am grateful for coming into contact with someone who was finally willing to push me instead of pat me on the back and tell me how great A,B,C is. I am just filled with gratitude, gratefulness, insight, and emotional exhaustion.

These are all quotes by students who have taken this class.

> "Dr. Cabouli's Advanced Seminar in Experiential-Strategic Family Therapy was, and probably always will be, the one course truly outside my comfort zone, while simultaneously being a major impetus to my growth as a person, and thus a future therapist who can be real and authentic with clients, as well as colleagues."

> "Dr. Cabouli claims that her goal is to push her students and clients beyond their comfort zones in an effort to 'create a level of anxiety and intensity.'"

> "St. Exupery wrote that 'It is only with the heart that one can see rightly; what is essential is invisible to the eye,' and this quote exemplifies my memory of the class."

> "This class was a challenging experience that will test the limits of a person. It took me to the edge of my comfort zone and right past it, into an uncomfortable place, producing some anxiety. It was a learning experience that challenged me to experience similar experiences that clients have when in therapy."

When was the last time you took a class and could reflect back on such emotional growth? How does this class work? What is strategic-experiential family therapy?

Strategic-Experiential Family Therapy is a five-part model, designed by Dr. Liliana Cabouli, which incorporates general system dynamics with strategic work. There is intergenerational work, meditative work. There is communicative work, as well as role-playing. Encompassing them all are the experiential techniques: sculpting, visual imagery, role-play, and relaxation exercises brought about by strategic directives that challenge and push the clients to change, be more independent, have more integrity and freedom of choice.

How better to learn an experiential model than to actively participate in it?

During the course of the semester, students are asked to push themselves to delve emotionally into their own family systemic dynamics through experiential exercises. The students learn through action!

This action can be, at the very most, scary; at the very least, anxiety-provoking. You must be prepared to examine yourself and your classmates through sharing and receiving feedback.

WHEN WAS THE LAST TIME A CLASS PARTICIPATED IN WRITING AN AGREEMENT OF PARTICIPATION, EXPECTATIONS, AND CONFIDENTIALITY FOR A CLASS?

That is exactly what you will do in this class. The first day, the entire class will participate in writing the mission statement for the class. That mission statement is then revisited throughout the course to make sure the class is achieving what they set out to do.

Dr. Cabouli is challenging, and the nature of strategic therapy is directive. Students are challenged not only to be the recipient of strategic directives, but are challenged to become more proactive as strategic therapists through the extensive role-playing exercises based on their own life stories.

YOU MAY THINK YOU KNOW STRATEGIC, BUT YOU DON'T KNOW EXPERIENTIAL STRATEGIC!!!

This class is going to be unlike any other class you have taken at AIU. The class activities will range from calm and relaxing meditation, to "in-your-face" confrontation on issues that the professor and other students witness. This class will be an emotional rollercoaster, if you allow yourself to trust in the process. The goal is personal growth. You cannot grow if you do not try new things.

REFERENCES CITED

Altarriba, J., and Bauer, L. M. 1998. Counseling the Hispanic Client: Cuban Americans, Mexican Americans, and Puerto Ricans. *Journal of Counseling and Development.* 76:389-396.

Auerswald, E. H. 1969. Interdisciplinary Versus Ecological Approach." *General Systems Theory and Psychiatry,* W. Gray, F. J. Duhl, and N. D. Rizzo; Boston: Little, Brown.

Bandura, A. 1969. *Principles of Behavior Modification.* New York: Holt, Rinehart and Winston.

Bean, R., Perry, B., and Bedell, T. 2001. "Developing Culturally Competent Marriage and Family Therapists: Guidelines For Working with Hispanic Families." *Journal of Marital and Family Therapy* 27, 43-54.

Bertalanffy, L. 1968. *General Systems Theory.* New York: George Braziller., 1968.

Bowen, M. 1974. "Toward the Differentiation of Self in One's Family of Origin." *Georgetown family symposium* 1:10-120, F. Andres and J. Lorio; Washington, DC: Georgetown University Medical Center, Department of Psychiatry.

Bowen, M. 1978. *Family Therapy in Clinical Practice*. New York: Jason Aronson. 1978.

Boyd-Franklin, N. 1987. *Black Families in Therapy: A multisystems approach*. New York: Guilford Press. 1987.

Brent, D. A., Holder, D., Kolko, D., Birmarher, B., Baugher, M., Roth, C., et al. 1997. A Clinical Psychotherapy Trial for Adolescent Depression Comparing Cognitive Family And Supportive Therapy. *Archives of General Psychiatry* 54, 877-855.

Christensen, L., Russell, C., Miller, R., and Peterson, C. 1998. The Process of Change in Couple Therapy: A Qualitative Investigation. *Journal of Marital and Family Therapy* 24:177-188.

Coatsworth, J. D., Santisteban, D. A., McBride, C. K., and Szapocznik, J. 2001. Brief Strategic Family Therapy Versus Community Control: Engagement, Retention, and an Exploration of the Moderating Role of Adolescent Symptom Severity. *Family Process* 40:313-332.

Colaizzi, P. F. 1978. Psychological Research as a Phenomenologist View. *Existential- Phenomenologist Alternatives for Psychology*. R. Valle and M. King, 48-71. New York: Oxford University Press.

Denzin, N. K. 1989. *Interpretive Interactionism*. Newbury Park, CA: Sage. 1989.

Duhl, B. S. and Duhl, F. J. 1979. Structured Spontaneity: The Thoughtful Art of Integrative Therapy at BFI. *Journal of Marital Therapy*, 5, 59-76.

Estrada, A., and Pinsof, W. M. 1995. The Effectiveness of Family Therapies for Selected Behavioral Disorders of Childhood. *Journal of Marital and Family Therapy* 21:403-440.

Framo, J. L. 1970. *Symptoms from a Family Transactional Viewpoint: Family Therapy in Transition.* Boston: Little, Brown. 1970.

Framo, J. L. 1981. The Integration of Marital Therapy with Sessions with Family of Origin. *Handbook of Family Therapy.* 1:133-157. A. S. Gurman and D. P. Kniskern. New York: Brunner/Mazel.

Frank, C. 1984. Contextual Family Therapy. *American Journal of Family Therapy* 12(1):3-6.

Graham, C. W., Fisher, L. J., Crawford, D., Fitzpatrick, J., and Bina, K. 2000. Parental Status, Social Support, and Marital Adjustment. *Journal of Family Issues.* 21:888-905.

Goberman-Cabouli.L (2003) Integrative Experiential Family Therapy with minorities:A phenomenological -Ethnographic Study. Doctoral Dissertation, Alliant International University , San Diego, CA

Hafner, R. J. 1985. *Marriage and Mental Illness: A Sex Roles Perspective.* New York: Guilford Press. 1985.

Haley, J. 1985. *Terapia Para Resolver Problemas.* Buenos Aires: Amorrortu. 1985.

Halford, W. K., Bouma, R., Kelly, A., and Young, R. 2000. Individual Psychopathology and Marital Distress. *Behavior Modification.* 23(2):179-216.

Hawley, D., and Geske, S. 2000. The Use of Theory in Family Therapy Research: A Content Analysis of Family Therapy Journals. *Journal of Marital and Family Therapy.* 1:17-22.

Hazelrigg, M. D., Cooper, H. M., and Bourduin, C. M. 1987. Evaluating the Effectiveness of Family Therapies. *Psychological Bulletin.* 101:428-442.

Ho, M. K. 1987. *Family Therapy with Ethnic Minorities.* Newbury Park, CA: Sage. 1987.

Kazdin, A. E. 1996. Dropping out of Child Therapy: Issues for Research and Implications for Practice. *Clinical Child Psychology and Psychiatry.* 1:133-156.

Kazdin, A. E., and Wassell, G. 2000. Therapeutic Changes in children, parents and Families Resulting from Treatment of Children with Conduct Problems. *Journal of the American Academy of Child and Adolescent Psychiatry.* 39:414-420.

Kempler, W. 1965. Experiential Family Therapy. *International Journal of Group Psychotherapy.* 15:57-71.

Kim, S. 1985. Family therapy for Asian Americans: A Strategic-Structural Framework. *Psychotherapy.* 22:342-348.

Kuehl, B., Newfield, N., and Joanning, H. 1990. A Client-Based Description of Family Therapy. *Journal of Family Psychology.* 3:310-321.

Liddle, H., Breunlin, D. C., and Schwartz, R. 1988. *Handbook of Family Therapy Training and Supervision.* New York: Guilford. 1988.

Lincoln, Y. S., and Guba, E. G. 1985. *Naturalistic Inquiry.* New York: International University Press. 1985

Madden-Derdich, D. A., Leonard, S. A., and Gunnell, G. A. 2002. Parents' and Children's Perceptions of Family Processes in Inner City Families with Delinquent Youths: A Qualitative Investigation. *Journal of Marital and Family Therapy.* 28:355-369.

McGoldrick, M., and Carter, B. 2001. Advances in Coaching: Family Therapy with One Person. *Journal of Marital and Family Therapy.* 27:281-300.

McGoldrick, M., Giordano, J. K., and Pearce, J. 1996. *Ethnicity and Family Therapy, Second Edition.* New York: Guilford Press. 1996.

McNeil, C. V., and Herschell, A. D. 1998. Treating Multi-Problem, High-Stress Families: Suggested Strategies for Practitioners. *Family Relations: Interdisciplinary Journal of Applied Family Studies.* 47:259-262.

Milne, J. M., Edwards, J. K., and Murchie, J. C. 2001. Family Treatment of Oppositional Defiant Disorder: Changing Views and Strength-based Approaches. *Family Journal.* 9(1):17-25.

Minuchin, S., and Fishman, H. C. 1981. *Family Therapy Techniques.* Cambridge, MA: Harvard University Press. 1981.

Minuchin, S., Lee, W., and Simon, G. M. 1996. *Mastering Family Therapy.* New York: Wiley. 1996.

Minuchin, S., Montalvo, B., Guerney, B., Rosman, B., and Schumer, F. 1967. *Families of the Slums.* New York: Basic Books. 1967.

Minuchin, S., Rosman, B., and Baker, L. 1978. *Psychosomatic Families: Anorexia Nervosa in Context.* Cambridge, MA: Harvard University Press. 1978.

Napier, A. Y., and Whitaker, C. A. 1978. *The Family Crucible.* New York: Harper. 1978.

Newfield, N., Joanning, H., Kuehl, B., and Quinn, W. 1990. We Can Tell You about "Psychos" and "Shrinks": An Ethnography of the Family Therapy of Adolescent Drug Abuse. *Family therapy Approaches with Adolescent Substance Abusers.* 275-307. C. Todd and D. M. Selekman. Boston: Allyn and Bacon.

Nichols, M. P., and Schwartz, R. 1998. *Family Therapy: Concepts and Methods.* Boston: Allyn and Bacon. 1998.

Papp, P. 1980. The Greek Chorus and Other Techniques of Paradoxical Therapy. *Family Process.* 19:45-57.

Pinderhughes, E. 1982. Afro-American Families and the Victim System. *Ethnicity and Family Therapy.* 108-122. M. McGoldrick, J. K. Pearce, and J. Giordano. New York: Guilford Press. 1982.

Pinsof, W., and Wynne, L. 1995. The Efficacy of Marital and Family Therapy: An Empirical Overview, Conclusions, and Recommendations. *Journal of Marital and Family Therapy.* 21:585-613.

Polkinghorne, D. E. 1989. Phenomenological Research Methods. *Existential-Phenomenological Perspectives in Psychology: Exploring the Breadth of Human Experience.* 41-60. R. Valle and S. Rhalling. New York: Plenum Press. 1989.

Rait, D. 1988. Survey Results. *The Family Therapy Networker.* 12(1):52-56.

Roberto, L. 1991. Symbolic-Experiential Family Therapy. *Handbook of Family Therapy.* 2:444-478. A. S. Gurman and D. P. Kniskern. New York: Brunner/Mazel.

Rogers, C. 1951. *Client- Centered Therapy.* Boston: Houghton Mifflin. 1951.

Satir, V. 1972. *People Making.* Palo Alto, CA: Science and Behavior Books. 1972.

Shrek, D. T. 2000. Parental Marital Quality and Well-Being, Parent-Child Relational Quality, Chinese Adolescent Adjustment. *American Journal of Family Therapy.* 28:147-162.

Sprenkle, D. 2002. *Effective Research in Marriage and Family Therapy.* Alexandria, VA: American Association for Marriage and Family Therapy.

Sprenkle, D. H., and Moon, M. S. 1996. *Research Methods in Family Therapy.* New York: Guilford. 1996.

Szapocznik, J., Kurtines, W. M., Foote, F.H., Perez-Vidal, A., and Hervis, O. 1983. Conjoint Versus One Person Family Therapy: Further Evidence for the Effectiveness of Conducting Family Therapy through One Person. *Journal of Consulting and Clinical Psychology.* 6:889-899.

Szapocznik, J., Kurtines, W. M., Foote, F. H., Perez-Vidal, A., and Hervis, O. 1986. Conjoint Versus One Person Family Therapy: Further Evidence for the Effectiveness of Conducting Family Therapy through One Person. *Journal of Consulting and Clinical Psychology.* 54:395-397.

Szapocznik, J., Murray, E., Scopetta, M., Hervis, O., Rio, A., Cohen., R., et al. 1989. Structural Family Versus Psychodynamic Child Therapy for Problematic Hispanic Boy. *Journal of Consulting and Clinical Psychology.* 57:571-578.

Stanton, M. D., and Todd, T. C. 1979. Structural Family Therapy with Drug Addicts. *The Family, Therapy, and Drug and Alcohol Abuse.* E. Kaufman and P. Kaufman. New York: Garden Press.

Waxlike, P., Bovine, J., and Jackson, D. 1967. *Pragmatics of Human Communication.* New York: Norton. 1967.

Weissman, M. M., and Klerman, G. L. 1987. Interpersonal Psychotherapy: Theory and Research, *Short-term Psychotherapies for Depression: Behavioral, Interpersonal, Cognitive, and Psychodynamic Approach.* A. J. Rush. 312-347. New York: Guilford Press.

Whitaker, C. A. 1975. Psychotherapy of the Absurd: With a Special Emphasis on the Psychotherapy of Aggression. *Family Process.* 14:1-16.

Whitaker, C. A. 1976. The Hindrance of Theory in Clinical Work. *Family Therapy: Theory and Practice.* 154-164. P. J. Guerin. New York: Gardner.

Whitaker, C. A., Felder, R., and Warkentin, J. 1965. Countertransference in the Family Treatment of Schizophrenia. *Intensive Family Therapy.* 100-120. I. Boszormenyi-Nagy and J. L. Framo. New York: Harper & Row.

Whitaker, C. A., and Keith, D. V. 1981. Symbolic-experiential family therapy, *Handbook of Family Therapy, Third Edition.* 187-225. A. S. Gurman and D. P. Kniskern. New York: Brunner/Mazel. 1981.

White, J. 1972. Towards a Black Psychology. *Black Psychology.* 43-50. R. Jones. New York: Harper & Row. 1972.

White, M. 1983. Anorexia Nervosa: A Transgenerational System Perspective. *Family Process.* 22:255-273

Wilson, W. 1987. *The Truly Disadvantaged: The Inner City, the Underclass, and Public Policy.* Chicago: University of Chicago Press. 1987.

Wynne, L. C., McDaniel, S. H., and Weber, T. T. 1988. Family Therapy and Systematic Consultation. Terapia Familiare. 27:43-57.

Printed in Great Britain
by Amazon.co.uk, Ltd.,
Marston Gate.